The Rose Temple

The Rose TEMPLE

A Child Holocaust Survivor's Vision of Faith, Hope and Our Collective Future

S. Mitchell Weitzman
with Lucia Weitzman

SOLOMON BERL
Washington • Baltimore

ISBN 978-09961177-0-8
Library Of Congress Control Number: 2015903027

Solomon-Berl Media, LLC
12129 Faulkner Drive
Owings Mills, MD 21117
443-334-5132
fax: 443-450-3984
www.Solomon-Berlmedia.com
Inquiries@Solomon-Berlmedia.com

SOLOMON BERL
MEDIA, LLC

Printed in the United States of America

For Paula and Joshua Weitzman
and Genna Edelstein.

From her challenging origins,
Lucia is grateful for both her
spiritual and earthly journeys.

CONTENTS

PREFACE

Ishould not have been so bitter, yet it weighed on my shoulders like a boulder. In my comfortable suburban Detroit childhood, most everyone looked a lot like my family: white, Jewish, and middle class. As children, we played catch on tree-lined streets and built snowmen on our front lawns. Whatever racial tension was taking place south of Eight Mile Road hardly affected me. In my neighborhood, I never heard a single anti-Semitic taunt.

The Orthodox Jewish day school I attended was small and nurturing. It too should not have been a source of resentment. Yet one day, without any apparent incitement, I assailed a friend and classmate. "While your family was comfortable in America during the war," I erupted, "mine was being wiped out in Poland. You know your grandparents. I don't."

In those days, before children of Holocaust survivors formed groups and wrote books to explore the common threads that bound us—such as being haunted by our parents' experiences; and sensing that it was our burden to somehow make up for their losses—I asked the "why" and "how" questions many of us did. Why did this happen? How could this have happened?

Curiously, I never recalled much, if any, embitterment from my mother, though she had every reason to be resentful. I speculated as to why this was so: She was too busy as a homemaker, or too determined to adapt and succeed in her new homeland. She would later tell me that she'd made a purposeful choice to put her past "outside herself" and lock it in a "vault." She only wanted to look forward.

That vault cracked open when my father, himself a survivor, died. My mother was fifty-three years old at the time. No longer preoccupied with managing his illnesses, and with my sister and me grown, she was now alone with her thoughts. And once again, she made a purposeful choice.

After a period of mourning, friends offered introductions to eligible men and the promise of a full social calendar. For the most part, she declined the offers. By then, after much self-reflection, she had begun to be pulled in a very different direction. Through dreams, visions, and writings, many peppered with biblical references, she believed that she was receiving Divinely inspired messages that spoke not only to her directly but to our world's collective future.

To be clear, this was a drastic departure from the mother I'd known growing up.

She always had a strong spiritual core, which I vividly sensed at the Sabbath table and elsewhere. I grasped that a sacred connection she had with God had somehow survived, and even thrived, throughout a life during which she had been given to a childless couple as a toddler in a desperate attempt to protect her from the Nazis, and raised as a practicing Catholic until reconnecting with the Jewish community in her early 20's.

However, there was never any hint of the spiritual/mystical journey that was to come. She was grounded and pragmatic. Her transition back to Judaism was born of circumstance. Yet once within the Jewish community, she adapted its practices and traditions as if they had always been her own. It provided a framework for her marriage; a foundation for raising her children; and a network for an active, engaged social life.

It was natural, then, for her friends and family to expect her to seek security and comfort with a companion after my father's passing. So her choice to spend more time alone left many friends and family, including me, perplexed. (She did not initially reveal the mystical experiences she was documenting in her journal.)

Once my mother did share those experiences with me, I was wary and occasionally protective, concerned with the reaction she'd likely receive from others. In truth, she was just as apprehensive, but she persisted, continuing to climb to new spiritual heights.

As she did, my uneasiness dissolved. She was shredding through labels that define and divide people. And she was defying expectations of what she "should" be doing at this stage of her life. She spoke about love even when recalling instances of conflict in her past. She was reclaiming her authentic soul. And she was doing so with a vision that extended beyond her, becoming a portal to radiate Divine light and inspire global harmony.

I began writing *The Rose Temple* as an admiring son. Unexpectedly, it turned into something more. My own spiritual sensibilities have developed, often in synchronicity with my mother's. It helped promote my own healing. And it has affirmed my role and even my duty to make this a better world.

The process has been joyful, challenging and intense. I still don't have all the answers to my childhood questions. But I'm not nearly so angry anymore.

NOTE: As Lucia's son and author of this work, I am part biographer, and part confidante. For purposes of clarity and consistency, the book is written in the third person.

In some instances the accounts in this book reflect history as transmitted by family members and is accurate to the best of their knowledge. Some names have been changed to protect privacy.

*Jewish mysticism teaches us that no matter how ill or spiritu-
ally disconnected we have become, within each of us there is
a part that always remains pure and unsullied and will call
us back to our center. This aspect of the soul, known as the*
neshama, *is our direct connection with the* divine. *When we
attune ourselves to its calling, the* neshama *provides us with
the exact guidance we need for our soul's evolution.*

— Estelle Frankel, *Sacred Therapy*

August 2011
NEW YORK, NY

Lucia Weitzman opened the book that seemed to purpose-
fully emerge from the bookstore shelf and narrowed her
eyes at the preordained page. The image, blurry at first,
came into focus.

It was an old black-and-white photograph of children, faces
drawn and forlorn, gathered in front of a concrete wall in an
unidentified place. The only adult in the photo was a shadowy
silhouette of a man in a Nazi uniform, half of his rifle visible in
the frame.

For an instant, Lucia imagined herself as one of those children. A moment later, the image seemed anything but familiar. When she glanced at the picture again, it was new and fresh, as if it had never before been published. Yet she knew that photographs just like this one had appeared many times in memoirs and history books.

Lucia drew a deep breath and let it out with a sigh, feeling her tense jaw relax. A question entered her mind—one that, inexplicably, had never occurred to her before, though there was every reason it should have. She captured it and held it close for the remainder of day. And when she lay down to sleep that night—her soul returning to its Divine source—the question traveled with her.

The next morning, she received a response to the question—a direction, really. She understood that she was to ask the question publicly, and in writing. This was the question:

God, why were You removed and not involved during dark periods on the planet, like the Holocaust, 9/11, and other tragedies?

Lucia shuddered at the notion of publishing this question—a private thought—to God. She knew it was not unique or original. Theologians, philosophers, scholars, Holocaust survivors, families and loved ones of those killed on 9/11, and countless others devastated by evil and tragedy had struggled with this issue in one form or another. It was the subject of innumerable treatises, discourses, books, and sermons over the centuries.

For these reasons, Lucia would not have chosen to present this question in the opening pages of a book. Yet it is the question she was directed to present. And, she was assured, she'd already been given an answer.

This assurance also gave Lucia pause. Who was she to be given an answer to a question that has perplexed mankind for ages? Who was she to tread on this hallowed path, to take up this task and address a matter better left to more qualified religious and spiritual luminaries? Yet refusing what she perceived as direction from the Divine was not a choice she felt she could make.

The following pages describe Lucia Weitzman's journey from Poland to America, from Catholicism to Judaism, and from suburban housewife to bold seeker of mystical truths. The clues given to her transcend religious boundaries, speak to choices between good and evil, and hint at the potential for a better world than the one she was born into.

At the conclusion of the book, you will understand why Lucia believes, unequivocally, that she was given an answer to her question. The answer may not be definitive or complete. It may not satisfy theologians, scholars, skeptics, or victims of evil. But it *is* the answer Lucia received and has chosen to accept. And to share with you.

PART ONE

One

September 1994
JERUSALEM, ISRAEL

A little over a year after her husband, Herman, had died, Lucia Weitzman stood in the shadow of the Western Wall, the last remaining vestige of the Second Temple, and wept. She was not a woman prone to crying in public, but somehow, amidst the shouts, murmurs, prayers, and songs of the crowds gathered at the Plaza at the base of the Wall, her self-consciousness faded and she felt as if she were alone in this holy place.

Her two children, Mitchell and Lisa, accompanied her partway to the Wall. But she'd stopped in her approach and asked them to wait there. She needed to take the last steps alone.

Lucia anxiously faced the ancient stone structure, waiting for something—perhaps an epiphany, a sign? Nothing happened. There was an overwhelming depth to the nothingness, where meaning and purpose and life itself seemingly ceased to exist.

A gentle, steady stream of energy flowed up from her torso. For a moment she feared it might gush into a river of overwhelming emotion, of bewilderment and grief, that she would be unable to contain. Looking down at the earth, she whispered to God, "You made me an orphan again. For the third time in my life, You made me an orphan. Why don't You take care of me?" She waited for a response. None came. Looking up, she fixed her gaze on the Wall. "I won't come back here," she declared, "until I am no longer an orphan."

Had she uttered her ultimatum aloud, or only thought it? She wasn't sure. She cast her eyes down, tears streaming down her face. What had she done? She had challenged God, had threatened to abandon Him.

Yet strangely, unexpectedly, she felt purged. She *had* been wronged. Life *had* been unfair to her. She'd never acknowledged it before—not in childhood, not in young adulthood, not in the course of marriage and motherhood. Now she'd finally admitted it. The injustice had finally been released, to be absorbed into the ancient crevices of the holy structure.

She stood erect and lifted her head, looking skyward. In that instant a light touch on her shoulder, like a gentle feather stroke, sent a shiver down her spine. God had touched her—she had not imagined that. And she was sure she knew what it meant.

If God has again made me an orphan, she thought, *He will find a new path for me, so that I will not be alone. I have to trust Him.* Her cry had been heard and would be answered. Wrongs would be righted. She would not be alone for long. She was certain of it.

TWO

January 8, 1940
BOCHNIA, POLAND

The existence of the State of Israel, with throngs of Jews worshipping at the Western Wall, was beyond even the realm of dreams in January 1940. In one corner of the forsaken world of Nazi-occupied Europe, in the town of Bochnia, Poland, Lucia Weitzman was born to Michael and Adele Berl and blessed with the name Rose.

Bochnia is a picturesque town of gently sloping hills about twenty-eight miles south of Krakow. It is renowned for its salt mine, located 820 feet below the earth, where an underground sanatorium and elaborate chapel, sculpted into the salt, have legendary healing powers. The Germans occupied Bochnia on September 3, 1939, and renamed it Salzberg, meaning "salt mountain."

An estimated thirty-five hundred Jews lived in Bochnia at the time, about 20 percent of the total population. In Bochnia and in towns throughout Poland, the Nazis quickly issued edicts designed to subjugate the Jewish population. In December 1939, every Jew was required to wear a white armband bearing a blue Star of David. In May

1940, a "fine" of 3 million zloty ($600,000) was demanded from the Jewish population. And in June through December 1940, hundreds of Jews were sent to labor camps and had to pay their own transportation costs.

An area encompassing less than a dozen streets was designated a Jewish ghetto. Between March and April 1941, all Jews residing outside the designated area were moved into the ghetto, while the Poles residing in the designated area were moved out. The electricity was cut off, food was tightly rationed, and sanitation was limited to outdoor facilities. Jews from surrounding communities were also relocated to the Bochnia ghetto, forcing families large and small to share ever-dwindling living space.

In July 1941, Jews were prohibited from leaving the ghetto without a special permit. Violations were punishable by death. Workshops where Jews manufactured German army uniforms, electrical equipment, and baskets were established within the ghetto. Other Jews were escorted out of the ghetto each day to perform forced labor.

Despite the hardships, the Jews of Bochnia coped as best they could and maintained a semblance of normalcy. Makeshift schools were established so that many young students could continue to study Torah and the Talmud, as their ancestors had done for centuries.

But in the spring of 1942, the semblance of normalcy came to an end as construction began on a seven-foot wooden fence surrounding the ghetto. Soon news of mass deportations and Nazi extermination squads murdering entire nearby communities reached an increasingly tense Bochnia population. The hope that Jews could continue to buy or work their way out of any dire straits faded.

Some began to build bunkers to hide in when the time came. Others contemplated escape. Michael and Adele Berl considered their options for themselves and little Rose, now two years old.

They decided to escape. But escape routes were few, perilous, exorbitantly expensive, and, in many instances, deceptive. Smugglers and officials who accepted bribes in exchange for protection sometimes betrayed their clients to the Gestapo. There was no way to be sure if an escape route would lead to freedom or to an execution line.

Still they had to try *something*. They planned on joining a group traveling via Slovakia to Hungary, where Jews were reportedly still safe from the Nazis. Duplicate certificates of Hungarian citizenship would be supplied to the escapees, who would then board a bunker truck equipped with a double floor. Escapees would lie between the two floors and agricultural crops or construction material would be loaded on top. If they made it to the Slovakian border they would emerge to present their Hungarian citizenship papers and enter Hungary. The plan seemed promising. But there was a significant problem: what to do with Rose?

Time was of the essence. The ghetto wall was nearing completion. They wanted to keep Rose with them, under their protection. But could they take a two-year-old girl on a covert escape mission through Nazi-occupied territory, when an ill-timed whimper could cost all the escapees their lives? In the end, Michael and Adele made a soul-wrenching decision: they decided to give Rose to a Polish family who would hide and keep her until they could reclaim her after the war.

Agneiszka Jaworski, a Polish Catholic woman, had been a good friend of Adele's since childhood. She and her husband, Sebastian, agreed to broker the escape plan. For their help, the Berls paid nearly all of their financial resources. They gave Rose to the Jaworskis in March or April of 1942. The Jaworskis then placed Rose with a farming family on the outskirts of the city.

The Jaworskis also placed another Jewish girl, a year older than Rose, with the same family. But the three-year-old would not stop screaming for her mother, kicking and banging at the front door to be let out. Afraid for their own lives, with the Germans actively seeking out Poles hiding Jews in their homes, the family sent both girls back. Rose was returned to the ghetto, into the arms of her bewildered parents, without the money the Berls had given to the Jaworskis.

Three

Late August 1993
WIESBADEN, GERMANY
TYROL, AUSTRIA

In the summer of 1993, a little over a year before her mystical encounter at the Western Wall, Lucia had also experienced a strange, even frightening, other worldly incident. She and Herman went to visit friends in Wiesbaden, Germany, where Herman had lived for nearly a decade after the Second World War. After Wiesbaden, they drove to the Seefeld Resort in the Tyrol region of Austria. It was a breathtaking drive through hypnotizing mountain peaks towering over grassy pastures and gleaming streams.

Herman, usually expressive, drove in silence. As they approached the Olympic village of Innsbruck, just before the Seefeld Resort, he finally spoke.

"Lucia, there are some pension transfer forms in my green notebook at home. Don't forget to fill them out when the time comes."

A shiver ran through Lucia's body. Herman's voice seemed foreign; its deep, throaty tone communicated love, yet demanded attention.

"Why are you talking about this now?" she asked.

"I just want to make sure you're taken care of."

Lucia nodded and they continued their drive in silence. They arrived at the Seefeld Resort at dusk. The desk clerk handed them a silver key and directed them to their room. The room was implausibly narrow and confined. Too small even to accommodate their luggage, it was hardly the "deluxe" accommodations advertised in the travel brochure.

"Should we leave?" Lucia asked.

Herman ventured across the room and opened a door onto a balcony with a stunning view of the mountains and a lake that left them both in awe.

"It's too late to look for another place," he said. "We'll stay the night and look for a larger room tomorrow."

They settled into bed, leaving the balcony door open. Lucia nuzzled against Herman as a summer storm unleashed spectacular lighting and thunder. Exhausted, her eyes grew heavy and she drifted into a deep sleep.

During the night she vaguely sensed a presence of some sort; then a white, misty, pillar-like figure entered the room through the open balcony door. A sudden terror overwhelmed her, and the misty figure dragged her, crying and struggling from the bed and across the room to the door. She awoke breathing heavily, her body painfully constricted. It was just a dream, she reassured herself.

"Lucia?" Herman lay awake beside her. "Are you alright?"

"Y-yes. I just had a restless sleep. It's probably the storm."

"You were having a bad dream. You were screaming, 'Don't take me away, don't take me away!' I thought you would wake up the entire hotel. I worried someone might call the police."

"Why didn't you wake me? Why didn't you help me?"

"I can't help you anymore," he said.

Lucia looked into his eyes for clarification, but there was none. The following night, Lucia dreamed that Herman died. In the morning, all she wanted was to go home. Herman consented, to her surprise, despite the substantial cancellation and ticket-changing fees.

Returning to Wiesbaden, on the night before their flight home, they joined their friends for a concert by famed opera singer Luciano Pavarotti in an open-air amphitheater. It was a beautiful, cloudless night, the temperature cooling comfortably after a hot day. Pavarotti was brilliant, eliciting enthusiastic applause and cheers from the gathered crowd. At one point, Herman leaned over and whispered gently in Lucia's ear, "I wish it would rain."

Lucia wondered why he would say that but decided not to ask. She hoped her dreams in Tyrol were just harmless manifestations of her ongoing worries about Herman's often ill health. But she also knew that something more was happening to her. She didn't tell Herman that thirty years earlier in Bochnia, she had also dreamed about a cloud-like figure dragging her from her bed. A short time after that vision, her life had changed dramatically.

September 1993
NEW YORK, NY

Herman was tranquil yet somehow also energized when he and Lucia returned home from their trip to Germany and Tyrol about nine o'clock on the evening of September 9th.

Lisa, their daughter, came by to welcome them and then returned to her Upper West Side apartment. Their son Mitchell, living in Arlington, Virginia, looked forward to hearing about the trip the following morning. Exhausted, Lucia unpacked her nightgown and readied herself for bed. Herman screwed in a doorknob that had come loose, adjusted a window that was ajar, and began sorting through the pile of mail that had been awaiting his attention for over a month. He looked invigorated by the trip, almost youthful, Lucia thought, as she headed to the bedroom and lay down on her deeply missed bed and pillow.

"I'm sorry I didn't get to see Mitchell," Herman called out as she pulled the sheets over her. "How is he?"

"I'm sure he's fine. Maybe you should get some rest."

Sometime after two o'clock in the morning Lucia groggily awoke, feeling thirsty. To her surprise, Herman was still awake, several piles of papers spread out before him on the dining room table.

"You still up?" Lucia mumbled. "Maybe you should go to sleep."

"I will." Herman hardly looked up from his papers.

Lucia made some hot tea, adding a drop of honey to the cup. Rosh Hashanah was only a few days away. She made a mental note to buy more honey in the next few days. She sipped her tea in the kitchen and walked past a still engrossed Herman.

"You really should get some sleep," she repeated.

"Stop pushing me to go to sleep," he responded gently. "I'll have plenty of sleep."

A car horn awoke Lucia at seven o'clock. She thought about waking Herman but decided against it. She went out for some coffee and returned a half hour later. She tapped on him lightly, asking if he wanted coffee and a blueberry muffin.

There was no response.

"Herman," she called out. He lay on his back, motionless.

"Herman!"

But he still did not respond. He was gone.

Four

1942
BOCHNIA, POLAND

In mid-August 1942, the Nazis relocated people from other Jewish communities to the Bochnia ghetto, swelling the population. The clustering of Jews in this confined area escalated their sense of collective urgency. Michael and Adele Berl still hoped their plan to escape to Hungary would materialize. They'd made the unimaginable choice to give away their child once already. Now Rose was back with them. What did it mean? Should they take her with them? Or should they try to find another Polish family to care for her?

One man who'd recently relocated to the Bochnia ghetto was Rabbi Shlomo Halberstam, the thirty-one year-old heir of the Bobov rabbinic dynasty. Michael and Adele approached him with their quandary, as other Jews contemplating escape with small children had done before them.

What to do? Their dilemma was profound. To keep their children with them was almost a certain death sentence. But at least their children would die *al kiddush hashem,* as Jewish martyrs. Yet give them to a Polish family and they might be converted to Christianity. That too would mean losing *yiddishe neshumas,* Jewish souls.

Rabbi Halberstam contested this view. "When even a remote

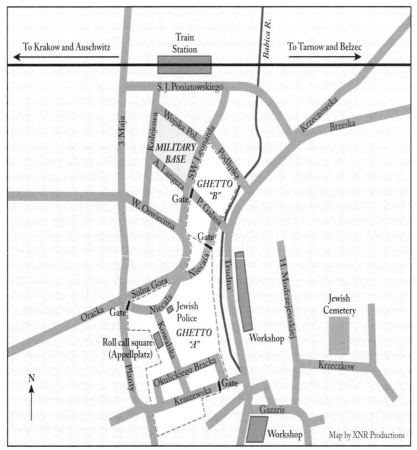

Bochnia Ghetto, 1942

possibility exists for saving a life, every effort should be made to do so."

Adele and Michael were not worried about losing their daughter's Jewish soul to Christianity. Their quandary was more practical. They'd given Rose away once, along with most of their savings, and had been betrayed. Now they lacked the funds to pay another family to take her in, and who knew if a next family would keep their end of the bargain anyway? But the Bobover Rebbe, as the rabbi was known, urged the young couple to try again, at all costs.

Shortly after this meeting, Adele contacted Genowefa

Swiatek (pronounced Sh-vyon-tech), a Polish seamstress she'd known for years. Genowefa had made dresses for Adele and her mother. Adele explained her predicament and her hopes to Genowefa. She confessed that she and Michael had no more money, but she promised to pay Genowefa and her husband for their help when the war was over.

Genowefa was a stout, middle-aged Polish Catholic. For years she had prayed for children, but she and her husband had been unable to conceive. They had informally adopted a neighborhood boy named Tadziu, whose parents had been unable to care for him. But Genowefa had always wanted a daughter. Now she told Adele that she and her husband, Franciszek, were willing to help, only they weren't sure how to go about it.

Days later an unexpected solution appeared, and a plan was hatched. Genowefa's niece in Stanisławów, who had recently lost her husband on the battlefront, was planning to visit her aunt in Bochnia with her one-year-old daughter, Alicja. Before leaving Stanisławów, the niece obtained a duplicate of her daughter's birth certificate, and changed the year and date to match Rose's age. If they could smuggle Rose out of the ghetto, Genowefa and Franciszek would announce that they had adopted a relative who had lost her father in the war. Rose Berl, the Jewish daughter of Adele and Michael Berl, would become Alicja Swiatek, the Polish Catholic daughter of Genowefa and Franciszek Swiatek.

One cool evening, Michael and Adele Berl dressed Rose in a white wool sweater and heavy beige tights and handed a concealed bundle to Genowefa's niece. By the time the bundle was unwrapped, Alicja Swiatek was in her new home on 1575 Krela Street, a dozen blocks away from the Jewish ghetto.

On August 25, 1942, Gestapo, SS, and Ukrainian auxiliary units surrounded the Bochnia ghetto. Those destined for deportation were separated from those selected to remain and work in the ghetto. The sick and elderly were transported to nearby forests and shot en masse. Small children were killed in front of their mothers.

After the August Aktion, about fourteen hundred Jews remained in the ghetto, including as many as four hundred who had been in hiding. Those numbers swelled as more Jews were once again relocated from other Polish towns and cities. The ghetto became a labor camp.

A second similar Aktion took place on November 10, 1942, after which the ghetto was again repopulated with deportees from surrounding areas. The ghetto was now divided into two sections. Those who were able-bodied and carried work permits resided in Ghetto A. The new elderly and disabled arrivals, as well as children, were housed in Ghetto B. Despite the ominous implications, a nursery was established in Ghetto B, a pretense of normalcy. The nursery would have been Rose Berl's last location had she remained in the ghetto.

Five

December 1993–September 1994
NEW YORK, NY
JERUSALEM, ISRAEL

Afterthe last lawyer had been consulted, the last insurance agent visited, and the last document submitted in the wake of Herman's death, an aimlessness compounded Lucia's heartache. Yet it wasn't so much loneliness as an unnerving sense of aloneness. She hated the term "widow" and had no interest in reading books about widowhood, stages of grief, or how and when to resume socializing.

Then one day she received an unexpected call.

"Lucia, it's Miriam." A familiar voice jarred Lucia's quiet resignation. "I just heard. . . I can't believe it. I'm so sorry."

Miriam Ferber, an old friend, had introduced Herman to Lucia. After a brief conversation, Miriam announced, "We're going to Israel for Sukkot. Why don't you join us? We'll be staying at the Tel Aviv Hilton—on the VIP floor."

Miriam sensed Lucia's reservations.

"You never know who you might meet, Lucia. Nobody can tell you how long you have to wait. It would at least be nice to see old friends again and maybe make some new ones."

Lucia softened to the idea. She was still a young woman—only fifty-three and looking ten years younger. Maybe, she thought. Just maybe, it's not a bad idea. Was it wrong to want a companion?

On the third night of her stay in the Tel Aviv Hilton, an elaborate banquet was held in the VIP room to honor an Israel bonds donor. Lucia dressed in a navy satin suit and entered the lavishly decorated banquet hall in slow measured steps. Burgundy curtains only partially obscured the view of the Mediterranean Sea, its waves lapping the shore below. Each round table was covered in white linen and adorned with gold-plated china and a bouquet of red roses. Miriam spotted Lucia from across the room and waved her over.

Couples quickly filled the tables. The men, smartly dressed with neatly combed silver hair like distinguished statesmen, and their wives, older than Lucia by seven or eight years, clinging securely to their husband's arms, raised their wine glasses to toast their hard-earned success. Most had immigrated to America in the years following the war "without two nickels to rub together."

A handful of couples gravitated to the dance floor as a four-piece band played Glenn Miller's "Moonlight Serenade." Lucia recalled how Herman held her on the dance floor long ago, his grasp more firm than gentle. The dance floor was his stage in those early years, and his young beautiful wife was his leading lady. But those days were gone.

"Would you like to dance?" asked a husky voice that seemed to come out of nowhere.

"Huh?" Lucia said, startled.

She looked up to see a man in his late twenties or early thirties standing before her. He had sandy brown hair and wore a plain white button-down shirt, khaki pants, and brown loafers. He seemed strikingly out of place in the roomful of Armani suits and polished wing tips. He was not the kind of man who would have drawn her attention. Yet as he extended his hand to meet hers, she allowed herself to be drawn from her seat and out onto the floor. They glided to the music, his arm firmly around her waist, his soft brown eyes gazing into hers. Slowly she began to surrender to the dance, and to the feeling of the moment. When the music stopped, she didn't notice. They kept dancing, now alone on the dance floor.

Then Lucia felt the eyes of the crowd focused on her. Their gaze jolted her.

What am I doing, she thought. Where is my self-respect? She blushed with intense shame. Thanking the young man for the dance, she excused herself and left the ballroom.

The next day, after a restless sleep, she surveyed the hotel in hopes of finding the man. Not that she knew what she'd do or say if she found him. She only wanted to understand why he had stirred so much angst inside of her. She felt again the pain of being left alone after Herman's death, and the fear that maybe she was destined to remain alone for the rest of her life.

She didn't find the man. She also sensed that what she needed now could not be found in a Tel Aviv ballroom, but rather in Jerusalem facing the Western Wall.

Six

1942–1943
BOCHNIA, POLAND

Though they had few resources, Franciszek and Genowefa Swiatek were determined to care for both Tadziu and Alicja, formerly Rose Berl.

Franciszek, tall and slender, had been a finance director for the Polish railways before the war. His work had once taken him to Krakow, where he reveled in the company of cosmopolitan friends from the city's intelligentsia, with whom he leisurely discussed politics and philosophy in elegant cafés. He pined for a return to those days. He had quit his job after the German occupation, refusing to assist the Nazis in any way. He joined the Polish resistance, often hiding in the forests and working to sabotage German communication lines.

Genowefa, a designer and dressmaker, had once counted many elegant women, a number of them Jews, among her clients. But the war had diluted her client base. A once fashionable woman herself, she had been weathered by hardship, gaining weight and losing interest in keeping up with the latest styles. She rarely ventured beyond her beloved church, where she asked God to banish the evil forces that had invaded her homeland.

But those forces remained powerful. A third Aktion began on September 1, 1943. On that morning, Genowefa descended the steps from their second floor apartment on her way to church.

She stiffened with fear as she approached a main intersection and saw several rows of men and women in the street wearing white armbands marked with Stars of David. They stood nervously at attention while German guards shouted orders in rapid succession. In the front line stood Michael and Adele Berl. Genowefa averted her eyes as she passed them by, praying they would not see her, that her secret would not be inadvertently revealed.

At church, she wept and prayed for them. She did not know where Michael and Adele were being sent. But she feared for their fate.

The third Aktion was an operation to liquidate the Bochnia ghetto. Only a handful of Jews were spared, mainly to clean up the corpses. Dozens of others remained hidden in makeshift bunkers, some small enough only to lie in, most with only enough food and air to last a few days.

The Nazis were patient, though. They waited quietly and let time pass. Eventually some of the Jews emerged from their bunkers thinking that the Aktion had passed, and they were met by bullets. Others remained in hiding, ravaged by hunger and thirst. Finally the Germans sent in dogs to do house-to-house searches, sniffing for scents, listening for sounds, ferreting Jews from beneath fake floor coverings.

Jewish children hiding with their families were often sedated with drugs or alcohol, or had their mouths sealed with tape. More than a few, weakened by hunger, died of overdoses or suffocation.

By the time Alicja turned four in January 1944, large signs posted throughout the city declared Bochnia *Judenrien*, or free of Jews. It was premature. Several Jews hiding in Polish homes were discovered by the Nazis or betrayed by neighbors and were summarily executed. Those gentiles who had hidden Jews were hanged in the town square as a warning to all.

Seven

Winter 1994
NEW YORK, NY

Lucia emerged from the Western Wall Plaza in a daze that lasted for weeks even after her return to New York. Nothing around her—not the buildings, the people, not even her morning coffee—seemed the same. Nothing was normal.

She told no one, not even her children, about her experience at the Wall. What would they think of her? Meanwhile she pondered the meaning of her experience and waited for the daze to wear off, to become normal again. She wasn't the first person to believe she had been touched by God. She had needed comfort, and had been comforted. Well and good. Now it was time to...

To what? That was it. She wasn't sure what it was time for.

She paced about her New York City apartment, enveloped in timeless days that seemed to have no beginning and no end. For years her time had not been her own. It belonged to mothering her children and caring for her husband. In her busy life there had been no time to reflect on her past, to dwell on old wounds.

Now she had no family obligations. Her days belonged to her alone. And yet she wondered if there would ever be enough time to find answers to all the questions that now consumed her.

What meaning and purpose did her life have? Why was she spared when so many other children were not? What or who was the misty figure that had come into her dreams, first in Bochnia and later in Tyrol, and dragged her from her bed? And what did it mean that she had received, or believed she had received, a Divine response to her anguished petition at the Western Wall?

Still reluctant to share these experiences with her children, Lucia felt like she had to open up to someone to alleviate her burden.

She met her friend Eva at an Upper West Side bistro. She wasn't sure whether Eva, who was not a religious person, would be receptive to her unusual experiences, but she'd been generous and supportive when Herman was ill.

She decided to share with Eva only her dream of the misty figure at Tyrol, not her experience at the Wall. Eva listened intently, raising Lucia's hopes that she could perhaps offer insight. Eva did not dismiss her or, as Lucia feared, tell her that she was crazy. But she did not seem particularly moved or interested either.

"Hmmmm," Eva said when Lucia had finished her story. "That was quite something."

"Well, what do you think?" Lucia, asked.

"I can't imagine what it must be like," Eva began, and then paused. "It's been over a year now. You are still in mourning. Maybe it's time for you to move on with your life. You are still a young woman. You should not be alone, Lucia."

Lucia was dismayed by Eva's response. Eva had told her to move on with her life? But she needed to assess where she'd been before she could move on. She would think twice before sharing her experiences with anyone again.

Eight

1944
BOCHNIA, POLAND

To celebrate Alicja's fourth birthday, Genowefa made her a white dress embroidered with purple and gold flowers. Alicja twirled about, giggling as the dress billowed out.

"You look beautiful," Genowefa glowed, lifting Alicja into the air. "Do you like it?"

"I love it. Dziękuję, thank you," Alicja replied.

"Now how about celebrating with a big box of chocolate? Would you like to come with me to the market?"

Alicja nodded excitedly.

Alicja wandered about the candy store as Genowefa gazed lovingly at her little girl. In the early years of her marriage, she dreamed of bringing a daughter to this very store. Now she had Alicja. She wished the circumstances had been very different, yet she could not help but feel a sense of blessedness.

The door to the candy store suddenly swung open. A German soldier walked in. Genowefa stiffened, her heart racing wildly. She hoped he would just buy a treat and leave quickly. But Genowefa and the little girl caught his eye. He walked over to them, bending down to look closely at Alicja. Genowefa braced her shaking knees. Did he know she was Jewish? That would be the end for all of them. The soldier reached into his bag and pulled out some candy, offering it to Alicja, who shyly put her hands to the sides of her dress and shrugged her shoulders. Genowefa took the chocolate and thanked the soldier.

"What a beautiful little girl," he said to Genowefa. And he walked out onto the street. Genowefa exhaled, taking Alicja by the hand. She paid for the box of chocolate Alicja had selected and walked briskly towards home.

Genowefa hesitated before taking Alicja with her on the next trip to the market, but finally gave in to her daughter's relentless pleading. They were on their way to the butcher shop when the sweet smell of apple strudel diverted them. They followed the aroma into the bakery where muffins, sweet rolls, and a fresh loaf of warm egg bread were on display next to the strudel. Alicja pointed to the bread. Genowefa noted the price, which was more than they could afford, but Alicja was now drawing circles around her imagined empty belly.

"I'll take one loaf," Genowefa surrendered.

Alicja twitched in anticipation, and Genowefa did not keep her waiting. As soon as they got outside, she broke off a large, doughy piece and placed it between Alicja's lips. It quickly disappeared. Alicja giggled and Genowefa plucked another piece.

"Challah!" Alicja said with delight.

Genowefa recoiled in fear. Challah was a traditional Jewish egg bread. She looked around. She saw no German soldiers. There was no one nearby; no one seemed to have heard. Genowefa gave Alicja an urgent look and put two fingers on her lips.

"Shhhhh, moya swatka. Shhhhhh."

Holding Alicja firmly by the hand, she led her home.

There were fewer trips to the market after the challah incident, and none to the bakery. Not until early January 1945, after the Soviet Red Army drove the Germans out of Bochnia, did Genowefa finally feel it was safe to take Alicja back to the market.

Nine

Spring 1994
NEW YORK, NY

After her disappointing conversation with Eva, Lucia sought solace, and then knowledge, in books. She began with popular authors like Deepak Chopra. Next she wanted to explore Jewish sources on life's meaning and challenges. But she found her lack of Hebrew knowledge an impediment to deeper study, so she eagerly enrolled in an introductory Hebrew course being offered by a local synagogue.

She went to the synagogue for the first session, but instead of the Hebrew class she expected, she heard a tall, thin, bearded man speaking about *sephirot*, which he described as a Kabbalistic notion of the ten attributes of God. The instructor, who'd introduced himself as Rabbi Cohen, described godly attributes such as understanding, symmetry, and infinite light, attributes manifested both in the physical and metaphysical universe.

Lucia was captivated.

When the lecture was over, a small crowd quickly gathered around Rabbi Cohen. Lucia hesitated. Should she approach him? What exactly did she want from him? She waited until the crowd dispersed. The rabbi glanced at his wristwatch, put on his overcoat, and started toward the door.

"Rabbi!" she called out. "Can I have a word with you?" The rabbi wavered. No doubt he'd had a long day.

"Sure," he responded graciously, concealing his reluctance. He seemed taller than he had been standing behind the lectern. He loosened the belt on his overcoat and leaned towards Lucia. "What can I do for you?"

Lucia stood silent for a moment, unsure how to answer. Perhaps this was a mistake. Yet she saw no graceful way out. So, softly at first, then with more assurance, she recounted her experiences at Tyrol and in Israel.

"That's quite a story." He paused, seeming aware of his poor choice of words. Then he spoke more deliberately, meeting Lucia's gaze. "Your experiences are obviously profound," he said. "But you need to be prepared to receive such experiences."

"Prepared? What do you mean? Read more? Study more?"

"Perhaps you should see a psychiatrist," he suggested.

Lucia recoiled inwardly. She didn't know how to respond. "I'll think about it," she finally said. Then she turned and walked away.

"A psychiatrist!" Lucia scoffed. "The rabbi told me to see a psychiatrist!"

Lucia sat in her living room beside Mitchell and Lisa. She had grown increasingly withdrawn since the Israel trip, and they were concerned. Lucia hadn't planned on telling them about her unusual experiences. But the worried looks on their faces, and Rabbi Cohen's referral to a psychiatrist, had convinced her otherwise. So she'd told them everything.

"Am I crazy?" she asked.

"Crazy? No," they reassured her. "We believe what you're telling us is real."

Lucia sighed deeply, relieved at their response. She wasn't sure how they'd react.

"It's okay, Mother," Mitchell comforted her. "It's under-standable that you wanted to keep this to yourself. I imag-ine many would call your experiences the hallucinations of a widow still in mourning."

Lucia nodded.

Before leaving, Mitchell had a last word with his mother. She'd been through a lot from childhood to now, and he won-dered what else she might be keeping inside.

Perhaps, he suggested, talking to a psychiatrist wasn't such a bad idea. It was not a sanity check. It was an opportunity to unburden her angst. It might even help her find the answers she was seeking.

Lucia reluctantly agreed to see a psychiatrist.

Turning right on West Seventy-First Street, Lucia glanced up from the pavement every few steps or so in search of the ad-dress written on a crumpled piece of paper she'd nearly tossed in the trash several blocks earlier. She turned into the doorway of a brownstone. On a black sign with white lettering she read a list of names, among them Dr. Stanley Rubin, M.D. Iron bars covered a small, cheerless window. She paused for a moment, squinting, then pressed the button beside Dr. Rubin's name. Moments later she was buzzed in.

Inside, a thin, distinguished-looking man, probably in his late fifties or early sixties, stood in the hallway to her left, beside an open door.

"Welcome, Mrs. Weitzman. Please sit down." Dr. Rubin di-rected her into the room, pointing to an upholstered beige sofa accented with soft burgundy pillows. Framed diplomas and certificates dominated one wall. In front of them sat a cherry wood desk improbably neat, free of any files or papers. Dr. Rubin pulled a leather swivel chair from behind the desk, angled it toward the sofa, and sat down facing Lucia.

"So, Mrs. Weitzman, what brings you here today?"

Lucia had no ready answer for this obvious question. "I lost my husband recently," was about all she could muster.

Dr. Rubin's expression showed empathy.

"How long were you married?"

"Almost thirty years."

Dr. Rubin asked a few questions about Herman and how she was coping with her loss. Lucia answered dutifully, if reluctantly. Images of Tyrol flashed briefly in her mind. She wasn't going to tell him anything about the misty figure she dreamed about in Tyrol. He'd be quick to label her crazy, she thought.

Dr. Rubin asked a few more questions about Herman, and paused. He swiveled his chair to another side of the desk, as if marking the end of part one of their session.

"Now," he said, "tell me a little about yourself, beginning with your childhood."

"There is not much to tell."

"I wonder about that." He placed his hand on his chin and leaned forward, waiting.

Unnerved by silence, Lucia began sketching her early childhood as she remembered it, and as it had been told to her by the Swiateks.

"Did your parents survive?" Dr. Rubin asked.

"No. I don't know exactly what happened to them. I only know they did not survive."

"What happened after the war ended?"

"I stayed with the Swiateks."

"Tell me about them."

"My mother, Genowefa, was an angel. I can't imagine any mother loving her daughter more than she loved me."

"And your father?"

"Franciszek? He was a noble man. A proud Polish patriot and an intellectual."

"How did he treat you?"

"He loved me too." Lucia pulled on the handle of her purse, hoping it was out of Dr. Rubin's line of sight.

"Are the Swiateks still alive?"

"No, they died many years ago, a short time after I left Poland."

"That loss must have been painful as well."

Lucia nodded. She could feel her eyes welling, and tried hard to suppress it.

"How was it that you left them?"

"It's a long story. The last time I saw them was on a train platform. We only had a few seconds to say good-bye. I had to leave the country and they couldn't come with me."

"I'm sorry. I'd like to hear more about that. It seems as if you've had a number of painful separations in your life. I think I can help you with the healing process. But first we'll need to go back to your childhood, to explore the roots of your pain."

Lucia glanced at her watch. "You know, Dr. Rubin. I think I am done for today. You have been a big help. Thank you."

"But we have ten more minutes in our session."

"Again, thank you, Dr. Rubin." She rose from the couch and walked out of the office.

Slipping into a crowded coffee shop on Broadway, she wondered whether she should have said anything about Tyrol or her experience at the Wall. She doubted it would have made any difference. She was certain that she was not going to find any answers at a psychiatrist's office.

Ten

SPRING 1945
BOCHNIA, POLAND

As the winter chill thawed, five-year-old Alicja was putting the finishing touches on decorating a doll house Franciszek had built for her. Genowefa had sewn tiny curtains for the miniature window openings and a new dress for Alicja's favorite doll.

Normalcy seemed to be returning as the war neared its end. Franciszek returned to work with the railways. Genowefa's customers slowly began placing orders again. Their tiny one-bedroom apartment was cramped—Tadziu slept on a straw bed in the main room just beyond the kitchen nook, and Alicja slept on a padded sheet beside him. But Genowefa was sure that better days lie ahead. For the first time in years, she dared to breathe deeply and relax.

One afternoon in the spring of 1945, a loud, nervous knock suddenly rattled the door. Genowefa cautiously opened it just a crack and saw a slender, dark-haired woman in her late twenties or early thirties anxiously stomping her feet. The woman pushed open the door and stormed inside. Genowefa and Franciszek had never seen her before.

The woman ran to Alicja and lifted her up to her chest.

"Rose, Rose!" she exclaimed.

Alicja cried, frightened of this strange woman. The woman put her down. Alicja ran towards Genowefa and clung tightly to her leg.

"Who are you?" Franciszek demanded.

"My name is Renya. Rose's mother, Adele, was my cousin." Genowefa froze. "In the ghetto, Adele asked me to care for Rose if anything happened to her and Michael."

"Do you know what happened to them?" Franciszek asked.

"No. But I have not found them. So I can only assume. . ."

Genowefa grimaced. "Come, moya swatka," she said to Alicja, who still clung to her leg. "Come sit with Tadziu on the couch." Alicja walked to the couch reluctantly, trying her best to understand what the adults were talking about.

Renya told the Swiateks that she had survived Auschwitz and now, several months after the liberation, was trying to reclaim whatever normalcy life might allow. To be honest, she told them, fulfilling her promise to Adele was not on her mind during the past few months. How could it be? After Auschwitz, how could she think about fulfilling promises to anyone? But a few nights earlier she'd been awakened by a chilling dream in which Adele emerged from a grave, covered in blood and sternly reprimanding her, "Why have you broken your promise to me?"

Shaken and haunted, Renya returned to Bochnia to look for Rose. She looked all through town, asking anyone she encountered if they knew where the Swiateks lived. She told them she was looking for a little Jewish girl who had been taken in by them.

Genowefa and Franciszek glanced at each other nervously. Who had she told about Alicja?

"Well . . . now that you are here, what do you want?" asked Franciszek sternly.

"I've come to take Rose with me."

"Take her where?" asked Franciszek.

"To be with her people."

Franciszek hesitated. They did not want to let go of Alicja, but they knew that one day something like this might happen. Was this that day?

"So you will take her with you?" Franciszek asked.

"No. I can't take care of her. I can hardly take care of myself. I'll send her to a Jewish orphanage in Palestine."

Franciszek stiffened.

"To a what?"

"I don't want to go!" Alicja burst out. "Mama, please!"

"Don't worry, Alicja," Genowefa said. "We won't let you go anywhere."

Renya protested but quickly gave up. Before leaving, she told the Swiateks that she had registered Alicja with the local Jewish social service agency. A package of food and clothes would arrive soon. Her pledge to Adele was fulfilled.

"Why did that woman want to take me away?" Alicja asked Genowefa, who was relieved that Renya was gone.

"It's something we have to talk about, my dear. I was planning on having this talk when you were older, but maybe we have to do it sooner than I planned."

Genowefa expected more questions but was relieved when Alicja decided she first wanted to play. She took her favorite doll and coloring book and walked out to the balcony that extended over the small backyard. Stroking the doll's hair, she began singing the same lullaby that Genowefa always sang to her at bedtime.

Alicja heard the sound of approaching footsteps below. She looked down over the balcony and saw their landlord, Janek Chmielewski, a red-faced, stocky man who usually gave Alicja candy whenever he saw her. He was grumbling angrily, his red face looked swollen like a balloon, and he had a brick in his hand. He looked up at her, then cocked his arm back and hurled the brick right at her. It passed by, just missing her head, and shattered the balcony window behind her. She shrieked in terror and crouched on the floor.

"Go to Palestine, Jew!" he shouted. "Go to Palestine!"

Franciszek and Genowefa rushed to the balcony and found Alicja surrounded by shattered glass and sobbing. Franciszek ran to the police station to report the incident while Genowefa attended to Alicja, who wondered what she had done wrong.

"What is a Jew?" Alicja asked. "Pan Chmielewski called me a Jew after he threw a brick at me."

Genowefa sighed. "Jews are people, just like everyone else. "Your parents were Jewish. And you are Jewish."

"My parents? I thought you were my Mama? What do you mean I am a Jewish?

"Come let's sit down, Alicja. We have to talk now."

Alicja listened intently as Genowefa told her a simple version of her life story. Alicja couldn't believe what she heard. And she didn't know what to think about it.

"Am I bad because I am Jewish? Does it mean you don't like me anymore?"

"No, of course not," Genowefa said softly, placing Alicja on her lap. "Jews are not bad people. Your parents were not bad people. And you are not bad. It doesn't matter what you are. We love you just the same."

Alicja had more questions but kept them to herself. Maybe Mama was just being nice. Maybe they weren't telling her the truth. Jews must have been bad, she thought, because the Germans killed them. Her parents were Jews, and they were killed too. So they must have been bad as well. And what about her? She also had to be bad, only she couldn't yet figure out how she was.

Franciszek returned home from the police station with a scowl on his face. He expected the police to arrest and charge Chmielewski, but they merely issued him a warning. He wondered how he would explain what had happened to Alicja, and he was relieved that Genowefa had already talked to her. Planting a kiss on her cheek, he whispered in her ear, "We love you and we always will."

Eleven

1995
NEW YORK, NY

L ike her conversation with Eva, Lucia's visit to the psychiatrist had been a disappointment. To whom, then, *could* she turn? Her children were supportive, but they were busy with their own lives, and she needed a regular outlet. One quiet morning it occurred to her: it was not some-*one* that she needed now, but some*thing*. She needed a journal to write down her thoughts. She felt compelled to write something down that instant, but she didn't even have a notebook or notepad in the house.

Grabbing an address book from the coffee table, Lucia turned to the lone blank page at the end of the book and began to write. She didn't know what she would write or why she would write it. But as she placed her pen on the paper, the words seemed to come to her from outside her consciousness. This is what she wrote:

> *The moment at the Wall was a monumental one. Only spiritual people with preparation reach the heights of God. You did that with the humble state of being an orphan. The gates of heaven opened up when you cried. You had to go through obstacles to come to your destination. There is kingdom in heaven and on earth for you.*

Lucia pondered what she had written. The words were powerful in a way she could not comprehend. How had the words come to her? What did "there is kingdom in heaven and on earth for you" mean? She was exhilarated, yet also frightened. What was happening to her? She paced the apartment, wondering if she should write more or wait for a signal of some sort. She waited in anticipation. But she didn't know what exactly she was waiting for.

Twelve

Spring/Summer 1945
BOCHNIA, POLAND

"I'm going out to play," Alicja called out to Genowefa. Genowefa was relieved. Alicja hadn't left their apartment for days after the brick incident. She hoped the police warning to Chmielewski would end the trouble and that a healthy color would return to Alicja's pale face. "Be back in a half-hour for lunch," Genowefa said.

Alicja walked down the stairwell and entered a narrow alley adjacent to Chmielewski's apartment. At the end, a gate opened up to the main street where Alicja planned to ride her tricycle. The alley was where Alicja sometimes ran into the landlord. She used to look forward to the candy he tossed to her through his open door. This time she hoped she would not see him. But as she passed the open door, Chmielewski was there. He grunted when he saw her and grabbed a butcher knife. Sliding his finger across his throat, he bellowed, "Didn't I tell you to go to Palestine, Jew?"

Alicja turned and ran sobbing back upstairs.

The next day, a notification arrived that a package was available for pick-up at the local Jewish agency. Genowefa recalled Renya mentioning a forthcoming package of food and clothing. It would certainly be helpful. Alicja's torn shoes, made of sewn

Post-War Poland

drapery and thin rubbery soles full of holes, hardly kept her feet dry. And food, in scarce supply even for the rich, was even more limited for a family living on the income of a government bureaucrat and a part-time dressmaker. Genowefa decided to accompany Alicja to the agency the following morning.

As they descended the stairs and walked through the alley, Chmielewski again reached for his knife and made a throat-slitting motion with his finger. Genowefa stiffened, clutching Alicja's hand. They hurried past the gate to the safety of the street.

Arriving at the Jewish agency, Genowefa and Alicja were

greeted by two well-dressed men exchanging papers behind a counter."How may we help you?" the taller of the two asked.

"We were informed that a package was waiting for my little girl."

"What's her name?"

Genowefa paused. She felt a wave of panic, instinctively looking about her for a German soldier.

"Her name is Alicja Swiatek . . . b-but you may have her listed as Rose Berl."

"Rose Berl. Tak," the agency official acknowledged, catching a glimpse of the quiet girl whose eyes carefully avoided his. "Here you go," he said softly.

He then escorted them out, holding the door open. Genowefa had worried that the Jewish agency representatives would ask about Renya or try to take Alicja away from her. But they made no mention of it. Her fears were allayed. . . for now.

Thirteen

June 1996
NEW YORK, NY

A year and a half had passed since Lucia wrote about her experience at the Wall in the back of her address book. She had waited for a signal about what to do or write next, but none came. Nor was there any clarity about the meaning in her life that she was seeking. Perhaps it finally *was* time to move on.

Friends had repeatedly invited her to join them on cruises. Men, widowed or divorced, were uncovered and presented to her. She had declined all such invitations. Now she pondered whether she ought to begin accepting them. She planned on calling Eva that evening but first decided to go to a bookstore.

There she stumbled on a volume by Julia Cameron entitled *The Artist's Way: A Spiritual Path to Higher Creativity*. It encouraged journaling as a means of promoting creative thought and contained multiple prompts to help in getting started. *A spiritual path,* she thought. That was it! A spiritual path was calling her — a call she could not ignore.

After purchasing the book, Lucia left the store. That evening, she held a pen cautiously over a blank page. Doubts flooded her mind. *What in heaven's name am I doing? I am not a writer. Who am I doing this for? Who am I fooling?*

She sat for ten minutes or longer, her mind drifting. When she looked down at the page, she was stunned to find that she had actually written something. Yet she had no memory of writing a single word. She felt both a sense of comfort and uneasiness when she read what she wrote:

God is leading my pen.

PART TWO

Fourteen

1945–1946
BOCHNIA, POLAND

The liberation of Poland from German occupation left a political vacuum quickly exploited by the Soviet Union, whose Red Army had driven across Poland from the east.

In what many viewed as an appeasement of Soviet leader Joseph Stalin, and a betrayal of Poland by the West, the Yalta Conference in 1945 sanctioned the formation of a new pro-communist Polish provisional government. Most Poles had hoped for a return to the independent prewar state before the Molotov-Ribbentrop Pact of late August 1939 had sealed Poland's fate. This German-Soviet non-aggression agreement had included a secret provision to divide Poland and several other territories into German and Soviet "spheres of influence." Now Poland's borders and demographics changed radically in the aftermath of the war. Its territory was shifted westward: Germans living in what was now Polish land were expelled to Germany, and Ukrainians living in what had been eastern Poland were now resettled in the Soviet Ukraine. With the near total destruction of Poland's Jewish community, Poland became an ethnically and religiously (Catholic) homogeneous nation state.

American-and Canadian-funded Jewish social service agencies were established in many Polish cities and towns. These offered financial assistance, sustenance, or transportation out of Poland to the relatively few Jews who had survived or returned to Poland in search of lost family, homes, and possessions. Some would be fortunate to find relatives in the United States, Canada, or other destinations. Others would be directed to displaced persons camps in the American-occupied zone of Germany.

Political infighting among communist, socialist, and nationalist factions intensified in 1946. The Polish population was already leery of displaced Jews returning to their former homes and reclaiming their possessions. But the appointment of several Jews to prominent government posts magnified that apprehension and fostered the perception that Jews were responsible for the imposition of Poland's Soviet-influenced communist regime.

As the tension grew, sporadic anti-Jewish violence erupted in dozens of Polish towns, often incited by "blood libel" accusations, a centuries-old myth that Jews ritually murder Christians, especially Christian children.

One such occasion incited a pogrom, a mass assault, in the city of Kielce. On July 4, 1946, a nine-year-old boy claimed he was abducted and held by a Jewish man. His outraged father reported it to the police, who accepted the account without verification. (Subsequent investigation revealed that the boy had gone to visit friends outside of town without his parents' permission and made up the kidnapping story to avoid punishment.) Shortly after, police converged on 7 Planty Street, a three-story complex known as the "Jewish house."

Police hinted to the gathering crowds that Jews were holding Christian children captive inside. In the next few hours, district police, local militia, members of the national Department of Public Security, and ordinary citizens converged on the building. Soldiers and policemen entered and shots were fired inside. The Jewish residents, forced out of the complex, were beaten and stabbed by the raging crowd. None of the police, military, or security forces gathered outside intervened.

Over forty Jewish Holocaust survivors were murdered that day. For most Polish Jews, the Kielce Pogrom was the final signal that they could never rebuild their lives in their former home. Most began making arrangements to leave Poland as soon as possible.

The Kielce Pogrom and the increasing violence against Jews throughout the country created a new sense of urgency in the Krakow branch of the Jewish Agency. Two representatives soon traveled to Bochnia for a visit to the home of Franciszek and Genowefa Swiatek. Their mission was to reclaim one of their own—Rose Berl—and provide her with safe passage out of the country.

Fifteen

June 1996
NEW YORK, NY

After reading *God is leading my pen*, Lucia found that she had written more. She wrote that this was to be a journal of personal reflection and spiritual exploration and she dedicated herself to the process. And there was a pledge to not write on the Sabbath, which is prohibited under traditional Jewish law.

From then on, she wrote in her journal regularly; it became her constant companion. She brought it with her to coffee shops, carried it on airplanes, and kept it by her nightstand. She filled pages with streams of thoughts, some happy but mostly melancholy. She recorded her dreams. Each night, she placed the journal in a safe and locked it.

During one morning writing session she was prompted by the book she had previously purchased, *The Artist's Way*, to write about her father. She read the prompt again. Was she supposed to write about Franciszek or her birth father, Michael Berl? She stared anxiously at the empty page. What could she write about her birth father? He was a mystery to her. She knew almost nothing about him. She had no idea what he looked like; there were no surviving pictures of him. His memory was as blank as the page she was staring at.

She knew a little about her birth mother, Adele. She knew some of her distant relatives had survived. At one time, in her early twenties, she'd searched available international registries hoping to find a surviving family member. She found none and quickly gave up.

Now, unable to write a single word, she grew restless. Finally, she left the journal on the table and walked outside. The journal remained untouched for the remainder of the day, and for many days after that.

But the blank journal page continued to distress Lucia. Had she tried hard enough to locate her father's relatives, or sufficiently questioned her mother's surviving relatives, in order to learn more about her father? By this time, many of those relatives had died, and there was little hope of learning more about him.

An uncomfortable feeling now nagged at her. Had she been angry with her father? Ashamed? Disappointed? A father is supposed to protect his little girl. Yet he couldn't even protect himself or her mother. And he gave her to another family. Other parents returned after the war to reclaim their children—why not him?

She felt her eyes well up with tears. And then she felt a wave of determination. She had to do something to fill the blankness of the journal page.

Sixteen

1946
BOCHNIA, POLAND

Two well-dressed men, representatives from the Jewish Agency in Krakow, knocked on the Swiateks' front door one early evening looking for Franciszek and Genowefa. But Franciszek had gone out to play ball with Tadziu, leaving Genowefa to answer the door alone.

Genowefa greeted them and cautiously invited them inside. One of the men carried a large duffel bag; the other carried a briefcase. Alicja ran in from the kitchen to see who the visitors were.

The man carrying the duffel bag spotted Alicja and smiled. He opened the bag and removed a princess dress-up set.

"Would like you play with this?" he said to Alicja, who glanced up to Genowefa's sullen face for direction. There was none.

"Is your husband coming home soon?" the man asked Genowefa.

"He'll be home shortly. What do you want?"

"Then perhaps we can wait. This is a matter of utmost importance. We'd like to discuss it with both of you."

Genowefa nodded.

Franciszek soon appeared at the doorway with a giddy,

playful Tadziu. They'd been to the soccer field and then to the market for dessert. Alicja noticed a white mustache streak across the top of Tadziu's upper lip, the residue of vanilla ice cream.

"These men are here to talk to us," Genowefa said. "They are from the Jewish agency."

"Very well."

Franciszek sternly faced the men. The man with the briefcase lifted it up and unlatched the lid. When he opened it Franciszek and Genowefa saw bundles of wrapped *zloty*, possibly enough money to feed and clothe them for several years.

"Alicja, Tadziu, please play outside for a few moments," Franciszek ordered.

The children walked to a small grassy area nearby. Alicja sat nervously under a tree while Tadziu energetically bounced his favorite red ball, oblivious to the danger facing Alicja. The men were after her; she knew it—just like the strange woman had been a year earlier. She saw the money in the briefcase. This time, she'd be given away. Mama and Papa didn't need her. They had Tadziu to care for—smiling, rambunctious, adorable Tadziu, who gave them no problems, who was not Jewish, who didn't have bricks thrown at him. Of course they would give her away.

Inside their home, Genowefa was frantic. "You can't take away my little girl—my Alicja!"

"They are her people," Franciszek said. "Do we have the right to keep her?" His musing was met by a steely stare from Genowefa. "Where would you take her?" he asked the two men.

"To a Jewish orphanage, where we have already taken other children like Rose who lived in towns just like this one."

Franciszek stiffened. "She has loving parents right here. Why would you send her to an orphanage?"

The men protested, but Franciszek made it clear that the discussion was over. Alicja and Tadziu saw the men walk out of their home. But she couldn't be sure they would not return one day to snatch her away. To be safe, she decided to never talk about being Jewish. And she would stay close to Genowefa and Franciszek whenever they went out of the house. As close as possible.

Seventeen

September 1996
BOCHNIA, POLAND
ISTANBUL, TURKEY

Three years had passed since Herman's death. Lucia had hoped for some sort of rebirth by now. *There is kingdom in heaven and on earth for you,* she'd been inspired to write. And at the Western Wall, she presumed that she'd received a Divine promise of companionship. Yet she had not found a companion, she still searched for answers about her life's meaning, and she still had not been able to complete the journal entry about her father. Finally, Rosh Hashanah loomed, with its empty setting in the dining room.

An escape from home offered a promising diversion. A friend invited Lucia and her family to join her in Turkey. Mitchell and Lisa flew directly to Istanbul. But Lucia decided to first fly to Vienna where her aunt, Vanna Swiatek, lived. From there, she and Vanna would take a trip to Poland. Lucia wanted to "find" her father, Michael Berl, she told Vanna.

Vanna Swiatek met Lucia at the Vienna airport, and the two women shared a warm embrace. Vanna's late husband was Franciszek Swiatek's brother. She had lived in Bochnia for most of her life but had moved to Vienna many years earlier to be closer to a daughter who practiced medicine there. Lucia and Vanna had corresponded regularly over the years, and she had visited Vanna in Vienna several times in the past. But this visit felt more like a mission than a reunion. They spent a short time in Vienna before boarding a train bound for Krakow and then Bochnia.

Lucia had been back to Bochnia in 1985. Mitchell, who had suggested that trip, accompanied her; he'd wanted to see his parents' hometowns. Franciszek and Genowefa had long since passed, and Lucia still ached at the memories of her life there. They stayed only a few hours before leaving for other Polish towns where Herman had lived and visited.

Now Lucia entered the train compartment and settled into her seat. She recalled how, over thirty years ago, she'd taken almost the same route in the opposite direction. Alone and frightened, she left Franciszek and Genowefa at the train platform on the Polish border, heading for Vienna, where she was to meet a group relocating to Israel. Vanna, sensing Lucia's angst, began stroking Lucia's hair as she had done when Alicja was a little girl.

After a seven-hour trip, Lucia and Vanna finally arrived in Bochnia. Vanna hailed a cab and directed the driver to take them to a house on the northwest edge of town. Relatives of Vanna lived there. Vanna didn't say why they were going to this house, leaving Lucia wondering how this related to her mission to find out more about her father.

A slender, middle-aged woman named Aleksandra Balik greeted Vanna and Lucia and invited them in for tea and biscuits. Lucia surveyed the home, looking for a clue. Photographs of Aleksandra, her husband, and two children were displayed in several places; a portrait of Mary, mother of Jesus, hung over a burgundy sofa in the living room. Nothing so far was even vaguely familiar. Aleksandra led the women to the kitchen where they sat at a glass table. After asking Lucia and Vanna about their journey from Vienna, Aleksandra said she remembered Franciszek and Genowefa — though not too well.

Aleksandra did not look familiar to Lucia. The name Balik was not a familiar one, either.

"I can't say that I remember the Balik family," Lucia said.

"My husband is a Balik," Aleksandra responded. "My maiden name was Jaworski."

Jaworski? The name struck Lucia with jarring impact. *Those* Jaworskis? She'd learned from Franciszek and Genowefa that they were the first family her parents had sent her to when they were planning their escape from the ghetto. The family that was supposed to have helped her parents but did not, and kept the money they'd been given. Lucia felt a sharp pain shoot across her head. How was she supposed to respond? Should she be angry and storm out of the house? Should she confront Aleksandra about her parents' sins? Lucia's parents might have lived, if only . . .

Aleksandra hadn't hesitated when revealing her maiden name, nor made any apologies. It seemed to Lucia that she didn't know anything about the arrangements between their respective parents. Aleksandra was only a teen at the time. But why had Vanna brought Lucia here? Didn't Vanna know this visit would upset her? Lucia was certain Vanna would never do anything to hurt her. Perhaps Vanna didn't know either, Lucia thought. During the war years, it was common knowledge that the fewer people who knew about secret arrangements, the better.

"Vanna told me you were one of the two little girls my parents took in from the Bochnia ghetto. I remember the girls. I can't believe you are one of them!"

"Two girls?" Lucia asked. She hadn't known that she was with another girl.

"Yes. Two. I remember hearing that one of the girls escaped with her family to Hungary."

Lucia grimaced. That was the same route her parents were supposed to have taken. She again felt the urge to storm out of the house, but she remembered that Vanna had brought her here for a reason. She had to at least stay and find out what that reason was.

"Do you remember my parents, Adele and Michael Berl?"

Aleksandra nodded. "Not very well. They were friendly with my parents. I remember that your mother was so pretty. I liked her clothes. And your father was very nice. He often came here and played cards with my father. He sometimes told me wonderful stories."

"My father was *here*—in this house?" Lucia shuddered at the thought.

"Yes. He and my father sat right here at the kitchen table playing cards. A different table, I think, of course." Aleksandra chuckled.

Her father was once in this very room? It was inconceivable, an impossible thought. Lucia tried to absorb the magnitude of it. She'd never felt his presence so closely. He'd never been so real. She suddenly missed him now as never before. She'd found her father in this Polish home, but now she wanted more. She wanted to know him.

Vanna planned on staying in Bochnia for a few days to visit old friends, but Lucia wanted to continue her mission. She wanted to travel to nearby Brzesko, a town about ten miles east of Bochnia, on the banks of the Uszwica River. One of the few things she had known about her father was that he was born in Brzesko. So she thanked Aleksandra and said good-bye to Vanna. Less than an hour later she was in Brzesko.

From the train station, Lucia walked about fifteen minutes to the town square. She sat on a bench, watching people pass by.

Closing her eyes, she tried to imagine her father there, to feel his presence. Nothing happened. There seemed to be no trace of him left here.

She opened her eyes again. An elderly woman passed by. Then she saw a father walking with his young daughter, holding her hand. Gazing at them, she felt a profound sadness and aloneness. Then it occurred to her; she was feeling her sadness, her aloneness. What about his? What did he go through having to give away his little girl twice?

She rose from the bench and darted for the train station. She'd done what she needed to do. Now she was ready to leave Poland and meet up with Mitchell and Lisa in Istanbul. After boarding the plane, she removed her journal from the carry-on bag. She was certain now that she would have little trouble filling in its blank pages.

Preoccupied with thoughts of her father, Lucia now turned her attention to the crowd approaching Istanbul's Neve Shalom Synagogue for Rosh Hashanah services. Lucia, Mitchell, and Lisa moved slowly with the crowd toward the entrance. Security was unexpectedly tight. They didn't know why until a gentleman nearby told them the story. About a decade earlier, at Rosh Hashanah, terrorists affiliated with a Palestinian organization had entered the synagogue and showered the sanctuary with a hail of bullets. Twenty-two people died. Bullet holes were still visible around the perimeter of the sanctuary. The bloodstained lectern where the rabbi had stood, left unrepaired, cast an eerie, unsettling feeling over the sanctuary.

The service was conducted in the Sephardic traditions rooted in Persia and other Middle Eastern lands. The prayers and chants were strange to Eastern European Ashkenazi ears, but the passion of the prayers was as fervent as in any synagogue.

Sitting in a women's section apart from the men, Lucia tried to quiet her thoughts. *What did this all mean? For what purpose is all this prayer?* And most personally troublesome of all, *God had touched her at the Wall, but why not since?*

She peered over the *mechitza*, the partition used to separate men and women, and saw a cluster of men huddled around the bima or altar. Children rushed forward in eager anticipation. A motion was made from the *bima* for a respectful hush. And then . . . T-e-k-i-a-h

A loud blast from the shofar, a ram's horn, echoed throughout the sanctuary. Once used in ancient Israel to announce the new moon and to call an assembly, a shofar is now used as a call to repent and as a reminder of the biblical story of Abraham's binding of Isaac to be sacrificed as a test of his obedience to God's will.

The sound of the shofar touched Lucia unexpectedly. She drew in a deep breath. She'd heard a shofar blast many times before, but this one was far different. She felt that *she* was being called, that she was receiving the personal response she'd long awaited—an affirmation that God was present with her now, in Turkey, as He had been with her in Jerusalem.

Eighteen

1948
BOCHNIA, POLAND

Genowefa rarely allowed Alicja to stray far from her sight. She walked her to school in the morning and returned at lunch to bring her fresh breads and pastries. At first the other children giggled at Genowefa's daily visits. But the novelty wore off and her presence became as familiar as the flags that flew in the classrooms.

As Alicja neared the end of second grade, Tadziu, one year younger, became ill. Now Genowefa's attentions were increasingly directed towards Tadziu. Tadziu had been everything Alicja was not: reckless, irreverent, and carefree. Now his boundless energy faded, he grew lethargic, and he started losing his hearing. Then he began vomiting and grew increasingly disoriented and confused.

The doctor's diagnosis was grim. Tadziu had encephalitis, a viral infection of the brain. His chances for survival were slim. Soon Tadziu rarely left his straw cot. Franciszek rushed home from work to bring Tadziu candies he could no longer eat and games he could no longer play. Franciszek could not fathom this calamity that had befallen the beloved boy he cherished like a son.

He hardly paid attention to Alicja, whom Chmielewski

continued to harass and threaten on her way to school. And he didn't seem to want to know about taunts from her classmates, who'd learned she was Jewish, or about her fears that men from the Jewish Agency might still be trying to take her away.

Alicja knew she was supposed to be sad about Tadziu, but she couldn't cry. So she rubbed saliva around her eyes to make it look as if she had been crying. She was torn. If Tadziu died, maybe she would be safe. Then she would be the only child, and Mama and Papa would not give her away for all the money in the world. Then maybe Franciszek would pay attention to her again.

Tadziu's several-months-long agony ended on June 25, 1948. He was seven years old. After he was buried, Alicja was moved from the sleeping pad on the floor to Tadziu's straw cot. She helped Genowefa change the straw, stained with Tadziu's last drops of blood and vomit.

Genowefa Swiatek with Alicja and her ward, Tadziu,
who died of encephalitis at age seven.

Alicja, circa 1945, at about the time she learned that she was Jewish.

Genowefa and Franciszek Swiatek, Alicja's adoptive parents, in Krakow, circa 1963. Their names are engraved on the Honor Wall of the Garden of the Righteous at Yad Vashem, the Holocaust museum and memorial in Jerusalem.

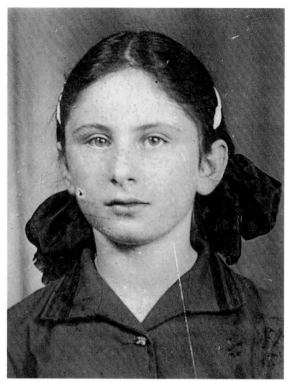

Alicja, circa 1950, at age ten, when coping with a landlord who threatened her nearly every day and classmates who taunted her for being Jewish.

Franciszek Swiatek, 1938. He resisted the Germans during the war, helping disrupt communications. When Alicja was ten, he took their landlord to court to stop his harassment.

RZECZPOSPOLITA POLSKA

Województwo ..małopolskie..............................

Urząd Stanu Cywilnego w ....Bochni...................

ODPIS SKRÓCONY AKTU URODZENIA

1. Nazwisko ....Berl.. ------------------------------

2. Imię (imiona)......Rose.. ------------------------------

3. Data urodzenia......ósmego stycznia tysiąc dziewięćset
czterdziestego /08.01.1940/roku ---------------
----

4. Miejsce urodzenia......Bochnia.. -------------------------

5. Imię (imiona)i nazwisko rodowe.......Michael Berl.. -----------------
(ojca)

6. Imię (imiona)i nazwisko rodowe.......Eidel Zollmann.. ---------------
(matki)

Poświadcza się zgodność powyższego odpisu
z treścią aktu urodzenia Nr ...2/1940

.....Bochnia...........dnia.14.09.2000r.

KIEROWNIK
Urzędu Stanu Cywilnego
Libusza Wojciechowska

M.P. PTH „Technika" Gliwice

Birth certificate of Rose Berl, daughter born to Michael and Adele (Eidel) Berl.

Lucia's birth mother, Adele Zollman, age sixteen. This is the only known picture of her.

The Bochnia Gymnazjum (preparatory high school), where after Easter services in 1955, Alicja faced a crisis of identity. She nevertheless continued to excel academically.

Alicja with classmates taking a break between gymnazjum classes in 1958. Her friend Marysia is at the far right; Alicja is pictured to her immediate left.

Director Alfred Bernacki (seated front row center) was the headmaster of the Bochnia Gymnazjum and a longtime mentor for Alicja. He was instrumental in securing Alicja's release from police custody in 1961. Alicja is in the second row, pictured behind him and to his left.

Alicja in 1961, just before leaving Poland.

Last photo taken of Alicja with
Genowefa Swiatek shortly before
Alicja left Poland in 1961.

Alicja as a teenager.

Alicja's Polish exit visa
to Israel, June 1961.
Valid for one-way travel
only. Citizenship listed
as "not established."
No return allowed.

A new home and a new name.
Alicja, now known as Lusia
Zollman, in Long Beach, NY,
summer 1962.

Rabbi Solomon Halberstam,
also known as the Bobover
Rebbe, was the scion of a
rabbinic dynasty originat-
ing in Bobov, Poland, that
relocated, after the war,
to Brooklyn. Confined to
the Bochnia ghetto at the
same time as Lucia's birth
parents, the Bobover Rebbe
was instrumental in urging
her parents to give her to a
Catholic couple for safekeep-

ing. Lucia had an emotional meeting with him upon her arrival to New York
in 1962. She would return to visit him often to receive his blessings.

Interior of St. Mikolaj Church (Bochnia, Poland), the church which Alicja attended as a child.

Interior of Tempel Synagogue, Krakow, Poland, scene of Alicja's first adult encounter with Jewish practice.

Exerior of Tempel Synagogue.

Nineteen

June 1997
RANCHO LA PUERTA, MEXICO

After the Bochnia/Istanbul trip Lucia spent more and more time alone reflecting, writing in her journal, and browsing through bookstore shelves. She often didn't return phone calls from friends. Lisa grew concerned about her mother. When she learned about Rancho La Puerta, a mind, body, and spirit spa located just across the Southern California-Mexican border, she thought it would be good for Lucia to attend a spiritual retreat there and meet people with common interests. Reluctantly, Lucia agreed to go, but only if Lisa accompanied her.

Lucia spent the day before their departure packing and meditating in her apartment. It was a gloomy, rainy New York day, and the thought of a sun-drenched retreat on the beautiful grounds of Rancho La Puerta lifted her spirits. Taking a break from packing, she closed her eyes, prepared to drift into a familiar peaceful place in her imagination of gently flowing waterfalls and lush, vibrant flower-beds. Instead she began to feel uncomfortably warm. She tried to focus on the inner landscape of cooling gardens and waterfalls that awaited her. Yet the warmth increased. Her eyes still closed, she sensed a golden ball hovering over her like a miniature sun, radiating a burning, blinding heat. She hesitated to open her eyes, fearing what she would see when she did.

When she rose from the couch, her first impulse was to cancel the trip to Rancho La Puerta. Perhaps her experience was a premonition: her plane could crash and burst into flames, or she could be blinded by attack or accident. She began dialing Lisa's number but then hung up as she recalled the words she had been inspired to write: *There is kingdom in heaven and on earth for you.* Why, then, should she be worried about harm coming to her?

Lucia arrived in Rancho La Puerta tired from travel. On the long flight, she read the schedule of activities and circled a mountain walk, a yoga class, and a guided meditation session. But first she lay down for a short rest in her room and fell into a deep sleep. Several hours later she awoke from a dream with a start. She got up and drew open the curtain of her room. She glanced up at the sky and questioned its ordinariness, though the expansive landscaped gardens, sloping mountains, and quiet meadows were exceptionally beautiful.

Now she took her journal and wrote down the strange dream she'd just had.

> *I was lost and looking for my home in an unfamiliar area. Several people emerged from a Yizkor memorial service at a nearby synagogue and I asked a woman where my home was. She pointed to my right. But when I looked in that direction, I saw a tornado fast approaching. I asked Lisa, who was with me, to take cover, but she refused. I looked again to see where the tornado was. But now instead of a tornado, I saw a ball of fire in the sky. I sensed, though, that I was safe in a sort of timeless protective bubble. A moment later, I looked up at the sky directly above me. When I did, I saw the torso of a lion hovering overhead, against the bluest of calm skies.*

Lucia paced about the room. What did all that mean? Why was she looking for her home? What was the protective bubble that preserved her from the surrounding chaos? What was the ball of fire, the second one she'd seen in a week? And what about the lion? She almost wished she was back at home with her stacks of books on dreams and symbolism that she could reference.

A knock on the door jarred her. Lisa had returned from a swim.

"Mother, I've arranged a massage for you in an hour," Lisa announced cheerfully. "Do you feel up to it?"

"Yes, that would be nice."

During the massage Lucia settled into a tranquil state, and at one point she felt enveloped by a blue light. She left the massage carrying the blue light within her. She had a feeling that it might illuminate for her the mystery of her dream. Ironically, she'd come to Rancho La Puerta, in part, to socialize with others, yet the events so far seemed to intensify her solitary spiritual path.

Twenty

1948
BOCHNIA, POLAND

Franciszek was inconsolable. For months after Tadziu's death, he rose at dawn to visit Tadziu's gravesite before taking the train to his job in Krakow at the finance office of the nationalized railway. But his workday in Krakow began to stretch long into the night. He usually came home after Alicja had fallen asleep.

At first Genowefa feigned sleep, ignoring her suspicious thoughts. But the fragrant scents that Franciszek brought with him from Krakow confirmed her fears, burdening her already heavy heart. Finally she could no longer remain silent and confronted him. Initially Franciszek was dismissive, yet his tone grew harsher with each confrontation, finally turning to rage. One night he struck her. Genowefa's screams stirred Alicja on her cot.

The next morning Genowefa put on a long dress, doing her best to hide her bruises from Alicja. She knew it was best to end the confrontations. Perhaps she had misjudged her husband. She recalled his nobility; after all, he took Tadziu and Alicja into their home. He'd resisted the Nazis. He'd refused to join the Communist party, though it would have meant a promotion at work. Now he had lost Tadziu, and she could not bear him a son. He must be frustrated, she reasoned.

Genowefa swallowed the lump in her throat. It was better to ignore his behavior and maintain peace in the house. For Alicja's sake.

But Alicja continued to stir anxiously in her straw cot at night. She knew what she'd heard. And she felt Genowefa's pain. She knew something was wrong, even if she didn't exactly understand what was happening. But what bothered her most was the realization that her mother was helpless to stop the pain, as vulnerable as she was.

Twenty-one

June 1997
NEW YORK, NY

After returning to New York from Rancho La Puerta, Lucia was unnerved by the lingering effects of the dream she had there. A tornado? A ball of fire? And then, strangest still, the torso of a lion hovering overhead, against the bluest of calm skies? What did this mean for her?

In a rare instance, she shared her dream with a friend and learned that the lion was a symbol of the tribe of Judah. Okay, she asked herself. What now? She walked into the nearby West Side Judaica bookstore, a narrow and sometimes intimidating place staffed with mostly Orthodox men seemingly steeped in knowledge she didn't possess.

She asked a clerk, a tall, thin man who struggled to make eye contact with her, whether they had any books on the tribe of Judah.

"Tribe of Judah?" he repeated.

Lucia wondered whether she'd asked a foolish question or whether he'd dismissed her inquiry because she was a woman.

Either way, she was going to find out more about the tribe of Judah and the connection to a lion.

The man motioned for her to follow him into a corner of the store. "We don't have a book on tribe of Judah," he said, climbing the ladder to the upper shelves. "But this book may have what you want." He pulled out a thick, hardcover volume entitled *The Shevatim: The Blessings and History of the Tribes of Israel as They Appear in the Torah* by Rabbi Moshe Polter. The clerk handed her the book and swiftly returned to the front of the store.

Lucia focused her attention on the book in her hand. She quickly leafed through the pages and came upon the section discussing Judah.

An image immediately caught her eye. It was a lion! Her Hebrew knowledge was limited, but she could make out the Hebrew lettering of *Ye-Hu-Dah*—Judah.

Her friend was right. There was a connection between the lion and the tribe of Judah!

She skimmed through the text. Within Judaism, the tribe of Judah is traditionally symbolized by a lion. In Genesis, the patriarch Jacob refers to his son, Judah, as a *Gur Aryeh,* a "Young Lion," likening him to the king of beasts, and telling him that he will be a leader of his people.

She read further: "The flag of the tribe of Judah was sky blue and pictured on it was a lion."

She felt a wave of heat flooding her face. The lion in her dream—against the bluest of skies.

Snapping the book shut, she walked to the counter, handed the cashier her credit card, and tightly held onto the plastic bag as she slowly walked home.

Lucia learned more in the days that followed. The biblical verses referring to the patriarch Jacob's blessings and prophesy of Judah along with the rest of his sons, the future tribes of Israel, are difficult to interpret. Genesis 49:10 states that the scepter of leadership shall not leave Judah and his descendants until Shiloh arrives. Some commentators infer from the passage a prophecy that comes to fruition with the reign of King David. Others, including Christian commentators, ascribe messianic implications to the verse.

Lucia was not eager to draw any conclusions. She was not a biblical scholar. Lucia felt that *something* was being presented to her in her dreams. But as yet she had no idea what it meant, or what to do about it.

Twenty-two

1948–1949
BOCHNIA, POLAND

Alicja's grade school was housed in a three-story, white brick building with pinkish tan trim around the windows and doorways. Every so often, when Alicja heard some classmate asking why a Jew had to be in their school, she stiffened, averted her eyes, and acted as if she'd heard nothing. Since beginning school, she'd sat in the first row of chairs, usually alone, until a teacher ordered other students to sit beside her.

At age eight Alicja was determined to succeed. Whatever the Jews had done, whatever her classmates thought of Jews, and whatever they thought of her, she would show everyone how good she was. She would be the most devoted daughter and be the best student in all of Bochnia. She developed a zealous habit of completing several days of homework in advance; the other students could not keep up with her. She often raised her hand to answer the teacher's first question, and she raised her hand to answer every question posed after that.

But while being ahead of the other students earned her the respect and adoration of her teachers, it only increased some of her classmates' resentment toward her. A few continued to follow her after school and sling slurs at her. She began to zigzag her way home to avoid painful contact with her tormenters. Her new path home took her up a hill into the cemetery where the children were reluctant to follow her. The dead would not bother her. Tadziu was buried there, but she rarely stopped at his gravesite, preferring to wander aimlessly among the unknown markers.

Other than the cemetery, there was no place Alicja felt happier or more safe than when she was in church. Franciszek rarely attended church, but for Genowefa, the church of St. Mikolaj was a place of spiritual expression, hope, and meaning.

Alicja would leap out of bed on Sunday mornings, awakening to the sound of the day's first church bells ringing from their belltowers. She eagerly put on her special white dress with pink embroidery and waited for Genowefa to get ready.

It was a twenty-minute walk from their home to St. Mikolaj near the center of town. It often seemed that except for Franciszek, every single person in Bochnia was going to church. A parade of men and boys in suits and women and girls in fancy dresses filled the sidewalks and roads. Offices and shops were closed. Only the churches bustled with activity.

Alicja would gaze at the soaring steeple above the three-story gothic structure as soon as it became visible. The sight was somehow both imposing and inviting at the same time, as if the church wasn't sure what it was supposed to be.

She and Genowefa would enter the open doors of the church, pass the vestibule, and sit in a pew on the right side of the sanctuary. Gently burning candles and the sweet smell of incense filled the sanctuary with a sense of impending blessedness.

In a few moments a processional of altar boys and clergy marched up the aisle and the service began.

In the name of the Father, and of the Son, and of the Holy Spirit. Amen.

Alicja rose when she was supposed to rise, and kneeled when she was supposed to kneel. She could hardly understand the parts of the service that were recited in Latin, but pretended she knew them anyway. Occasionally the priest, as part of the homily, would mention something about Jews. Alicja usually drifted off into her own thoughts during the homily. Whatever was said was usually intended for the adults.

Sometimes she would just gaze at the figure on the large cross over the altar or survey the pictures and plaques depicting the stations of the cross that adorned the walls all around them. How Jesus had suffered. How she had suffered. Who else could really understand her?

The hymns, Eucharist and Communion rites would soon call her attention back to the service. But it was what the priests would often quote from scripture that most resonated with her. "Love one another," Jesus said, "Just as I have loved you."

Jesus was all about love—and she was certain that he loved her.

Unbeknownst to Genowefa, Alicja began slipping into church on school-day mornings, where a devout few would gather for the weekday services. It was in church that she asked for the strength to boldly march to the front of her classroom. And it was in church that she asked for the blessings of peace to return to her home. Jesus, her friend and protector, could do that with his love.

Twenty-three

October 1997
NEW YORK, NY

A year after the trip to Poland and Turkey, Lucia no longer felt the urge to escape from home for the approaching High Holiday season. She walked to New York's Fifth Avenue Synagogue, squeezing by an elderly, fashionably dressed woman to reach her assigned seat.

The Rosh Hashanah service was already underway, the melodic chant of the liturgy beckoning her into its mood and spirit. The synagogue's cantor, Joseph Malovany, had a deep, penetrating baritone voice that lifted the letters and words from the pages of the *Machzor* and sent them soaring throughout the sanctuary and into the heavens. Lucia soon found herself enveloped in a kind of warm, spiritual cloud. Her attention drifted from the prayer book and she gently closed it, holding it in her hands. Her eyes settled inward, and she divined to compose her own prayers.

She prayed for her children; she prayed for herself, and for the first time, she prayed for her father, Michael Berl. Closing her eyes, she imagined her body and soul receptive to heavenly communication.

To her astonishment, she heard a voice—a male voice—say, "Thank you." Could it be? Was it her father's voice? She looked around her. There were no males in the women's section, of course. For an instant, she contemplated asking her neighbor if she had heard anything but decided against it. *Had she imagined it?* "No," she said under her breath. She could not dismiss this incident any more than she could her experience in Jerusalem. Could she now doubt that she had heard her father thank her as clearly as she now heard Cantor Malovany chanting another holiday melody?

She tried to steady her spirit on the long walk home to the Upper West Side, but it was a futile effort. She'd felt the way she had when she left the Western Wall. Her eyes seemed to see through her immediate surroundings, into a dimension of spirit that transcended space and time. She was embarking on an entirely new phase of her journey.

Twenty-four

1950
BOCHNIA, POLAND

By the time Alicja turned ten, she had mostly grown numb to her landlord Chmielewski's hateful ranting. But one day he seemed especially enraged as she passed him on her way home from school. For whatever reason, he lunged toward her with his butcher's knife and waved it close to her throat. Alicja screamed, and Genowefa came bursting down the stairs to the gate. Chmielewski glared at her and fumed, "Why don't you go with the Jew to Palestine, or Israel—whatever they call it now?"

Franciszek could stand by no longer. He filed a lawsuit against Chmielewski in Krakow. On their day in court, Alicja stepped up to the witness stand and sank deep into the tan, vinyl chair. Her feet dangled nervously several feet above the floor.

Franciszek, unable to afford a proper attorney, acted as his own. He presented the charge of attempted assault and recounted the numerous instances of Chmielewski's threats. When Franciszek stopped speaking, Alicja looked up from her chair and saw a tall man with closely cropped black hair and a stern face slowly approaching her. She glanced at Franciszek, who nodded, projecting confidence. The case was iron clad, he'd assured her on their way to Krakow. Chmielewski would not be bothering Alicja again.

But the defense counsel's expression and tone of voice—his tall body hovering menacingly over her—disabled her protective shield. His cross-examination was rapid-fire; the judge was not inclined to intervene.

"Did Pan Chmielewski ever actually attack you?"

"No. But he did throw—"

"Just answer the question. Did the defendant actually touch you?"

"N-no."

"Thank you."

"In fact, didn't Pan Chmielewski give you candy when you were a little girl?"

"I guess—I can't remember."

"You can't remember! Then what makes you think you can remember anything?"

"Uh—"

"You have quite an imagination, don't you?"

"B-but he called me Jew, and told me to go to Palestine."

"Are you saying he has something against Jews?"

"Yes."

"Is he allowing you to live in his complex?"

"Yes."

"Does that sound like a man who has something against Jews?"

"No, I mean, yes. I don't know."

"Haven't you always been a Jew?"

"Y-yes. I guess."

"And hasn't Pan Chmielewski always allowed you to live in his building, under his roof, since you were two years old?"

Alicja's eyes welled up with tears. She dared not look at Franciszek.

"Answer the question. Why has a man who supposedly hated Jews enough to threaten one allowed you to live under his roof?"

"He—He—I—I don't know."

"No further questions."

Alicja wasn't quite sure what was worse—hearing the words "case dismissed" from the judge or facing the wrath of Franciszek for messing up on the stand. Neither was a pleasant outcome for her.

The next morning, Alicja prayed, as usual, at St. Mikilaj. She needed Jesus's blessings and protection more than ever. She absorbed his strength and carried it inside her.

By the end of the school year, Alicja was presented with an achievement award, and at the beginning of the next year, she was nominated by the faculty to be class president. If some were left to wonder how she accomplished these feats, Alicja was not one of them. She knew the source of her inner strength, the one who helped her through the trials of her difficult life.

Twenty-five

July 1998
NEW YORK, NY

L ucia welcomed a new member of the family when Mitchell married in March 1998. His wife, Beverly, had been raised in a traditional Jewish home in Pittsburgh.

"She's an absolutely beautiful bride," Lucia gushed.

By July 1998 the couple had moved to Arlington, Virginia, and Beverly was pregnant with a girl they would name Paula. Now Lucia looked forward to Lisa settling down.

Lisa had been seeing an entertainment lawyer from Los Angeles on and off for several months, and she invited Lucia to meet him while he was visiting New York. They met for lunch in an Upper West Side restaurant.

"Mother, I'd like you to meet David Bass," Lisa said proudly; she also hoped for some relief from her mother's concerned scrutiny about her love life.

"It's wonderful to finally meet you," said David. He'd learned a bit about Lucia's story from Lisa and was interested in learning more. He was particularly curious about one thing: how had Lucia returned to Judaism after being raised a Catholic?

"How did you make that transition?" he asked Lucia across their restaurant table.

It was a question she'd been asked from time to time. And she had a prepared answer.

"I've always been a believer in God," she said. "My religion changed, but my belief in God never did."

But David's next question sent blood rushing to her face.

"What did you do about Jesus?"

Lucia froze.

"I ... I don't know."

It was such a simple, obvious question. Many people who knew a little about her background asked about her transition to Judaism from Catholicism, but few had ever asked her about Jesus as starkly as David just had. David sensed Lucia's discomfort and pressed no further.

Lucia left the restaurant with memories of St. Mikolaj and Jesus flooding through her, unexpectedly released from some inner vault.

A week after her exchange with David Bass, Lucia felt restless. She walked to synagogue on a balmy Saturday morning, yet felt uneasy there as well. She returned home before the conclusion of services.

She set her sweat-soaked blazer on the foyer credenza, turned on the air conditioning unit, and lay down on the couch. She soon drifted into a dreamy haze.

She was lying near a shoreline. Two figures appeared, slowly rising above the water, surrounded in a circle of bright golden light. Lucia's eyes followed them intently. The figure on her left had white wings; the other figure was cloaked in a long white robe. She could not see their faces. In an instant, they shot up to the sky, still framed within the circle of golden light. The cloaked figure briefly turned his head toward her and seemed to acknowledge her. Then both figures shot back down towards her, like missiles.

Lucia opened her eyes. Her head throbbed with heat and pain. She tapped her feet as if to assure herself that she was awake and alive, that she'd survived the encounter. The discomfort subsided in a few minutes, but all that day and into the next she felt that a golden light was surrounding her. She contemplated her vision, as unexpected as the memories that had flooded through her after her lunch with David and Lisa. Who was the cloaked figure? She knew, yet dared not utter his name.

But her pen would not be silent. In her next journal entry, she was inspired to write:

> *I was holding your hand so you would feel protected and secure. You trusted and believed in me. Your soul was pure and innocent, your prayers sincere. You forgot about your friend who walked with you all those years. It was not necessary to do that. You denied a truth about a part of your life that was important to your path. I came with an angel to show you that you have love and protection from heaven.*

Lucia was stunned by what she'd written. These were not her words. They'd originated as a thought—perceived or sensed as a voice she believed to be Divine—compelling her to write down exactly what was being communicated.

She had accepted, if not fully embraced, her developing spiritual sensibilities, but this was too much.

Unprepared to address the cloaked figure, Lucia focused instead on the winged angel in her vision. Who was he? She was drawn to open the *Dictionary of Angels* by Gustav Davidson. There she saw a familiar image.

She hadn't seen the face of the angel in her dream vision, so she couldn't say with certainly that this was *the* angel. But this was the only angel in the book pictured within a large circle of light, and the angel's wings looked like those she'd seen in her vision. This angel was actually an archangel named Uriel. The name Uriel, she read further, derived from two Hebrew words, אור + אל. The two words are *Or*, for light or fire; and *El*, one of the names for God.

Her dreams and inspired writings were becoming more mysterious, and their subject matter was becoming more sacred, if not fearsome. Yet Lucia was comforted by the thought that she was held in a circle of light.

Twenty-six

1952–1954
BOCHNIA, POLAND

It was as if Alicja had changed in the blink of an eye. Her thick white tights were outgrown. Her pigtails longed to be untied. Her hand, which Genowefa still held when they walked or prayed together, had grown larger, more feminine, her fingers long and slender. Her body was also developing, a bit faster than her classmates, as if to catch up with her accelerated emotional maturity. Had there been any boys in her all-girl classes, they surely would have taken an interest in her blossoming womanhood.

Franciszek, who had been distant from Alicja ever since Tadziu died, now started to notice her again. One Saturday morning when Genowefa went out to buy material for a dress, Franciszek asked Alicja to come sit close to him. He was sitting on their frayed, beige couch, a large, hardcover book resting on his lap. His invitation was as welcome to Alicja as it was unexpected. She darted to the couch.

"I bought this in Krakow," he said to Alicja, who eagerly nuzzled beside him.

The book, *Zagadnienia Seksualne,* had a full-color cover illustration of an elegantly dressed man and woman embracing each other. Alicja liked the illustration. Heartened at her appreciation, Franciszek flipped through the book, turning to a page that showed pictures of naked male and female bodies. Alicja looked away. Franciszek gently stroked her hair, nudging her head to his chest. He turned to another page, massaging her shoulder as he read aloud a paragraph about the pleasure of touching. Alicja felt sweat dripping from her armpits; her legs twitched nervously. She wasn't sure what to make of this. She was starved for Franciszek's attention, but this did not feel right. Still, she sat with him while he turned the pages and stroked her shoulders. She could not move. She could not hurt him by leaving the couch. He was being so loving, and he had paid hardly any attention to her for so long. But she hoped that her Mama would come home soon.

After that incident, Alicja, as she sometimes did, took out an old photo album on the bottom of Genowefa's nightstand to look at the pictures. Those old photos told a very different story of Genowefa and Franciszek than the one Alicja had witnessed for many years. They showed a younger happier couple, smiling and holding hands in various settings, and even dancing together.

In the photos Genowefa was thinner, her facial features were sharper, and she wore earrings! Alicja had never seen Genowefa wear earrings. Franciszek looked much the same as he did now, a handsome, distinguished man immaculately dressed and groomed, like Humphrey Bogart in those American movies.

Looking through the album, Alicja shook her head as a thought that had occurred to her many times before returned with a feeling of certainty. Perhaps *she* was the cause of the problems in the house. Perhaps she had come between them.

Twenty-seven

May 1999
NEW YORK, NY

Lucia was beginning to sense, in some small way, a light be-ing cast upon her journey. But she still had no idea where it would lead. After her vision of the cloaked figure and the angel, she continued to meditate, write in her journal, and record her dreams, not knowing what they meant.

In the hours before the Sabbath, which in this year coin-cided with Shavuot, a holiday with an agricultural component (commemorating the time when the first fruits were harvested and brought to the Jerusalem Temple) and an historical one (celebrating the giving of the Torah at Mount Sinai), she was inspired to write in her journal:

> *Be aware of your steps as they are guided through your dreams.*
> *Believe in the power of your soul.*
> *Shabbat is the key more than anything else.*
> *There is no substitute for Shabbat.*
> *That is the one day for God and God deserves His day.*
> *You need to understand about God's will and God's rules.*
> *God listens to your thoughts, which are the language of your soul.*

Lucia felt an extraordinary power in this message that had come through her. She planned to continue her spiritual work after the holiday. But on Shavuot she met a man named Fred Berger.

Fred Berger had seen Lucia at synagogue several times before, occasionally in the company of her tall, dark-haired daughter. She was, he guessed, a widow, or perhaps divorced. On this day, at the *kiddush* that followed services, he introduced himself.

He was a handsome man, Lucia thought, nicely dressed in a navy suit. Soon they began going out for dinner and attending Broadway performances. Fred was older, close to Herman's age, yet had a youthful zest and refreshing sense of humor. Born in Berlin, Germany, he and his parents had survived the war and immigrated to Brooklyn in the 1950s. Lucia felt a familiar comfort in his company, and company was nice for a woman who spent most of her time alone with her thoughts and her journal.

But Fred quickly grew frustrated. Still a bachelor in his sixties, he was enamored with Lucia, who inspired in him a desire to finally commit to marriage. But Lucia did not reciprocate his feelings. She needed a man who understood her inner life, who valued a woman who had visions of lions in blue skies and angels and white-robed figures in spheres of golden light.

Fred Berger was not that man. He made a disparaging comment on one of their outings about how "the *goyim* drink." How she *hated* that word describing non-Jews.. He meant no particular harm. It rolled naturally off his tongue. But for Lucia it reflected an attitude far from her heart; it was no different than a Polish peasant casually mocking a Jew. It bothered her. And it distanced her from him.

And yet, she wanted to be with him, to enjoy his company.

"Lisa," Lucia moaned over coffee at the French Roast on Broadway. "I feel like I'm in this big void."

"What do you mean—void?"

"I feel like I'm caught between two dimensions. In one dimension, I'm calling my friends, seeing Freddy, and going window-shopping on Madison Avenue. And in the other dimension, I'm reading, meditating, and journaling, having dreams and visions, and going…" Lucia paused, uncertain.

"Where?" Lisa asked.

"That's just it. I don't know *where* I'm going. But I know that wherever it *is* that I'm going, it's a place beyond where I am now."

Twenty-eight

June 1954
BOCHNIA, POLAND

After the incident on the couch with Franciszek, Alicja tried her best not to be home alone with him. But sometimes it was unavoidable. One day Genowefa went to the doctor's office, feeling pains in her chest, leaving Alicja and Franciszek at home.

"You remember that it's your Name Day, don't you?" Franciszek called out to Alicja, who was doing her math homework at the kitchen table. Every year she looked forward to June 21st, the day celebrated by all girls and women in Poland named Alicja. June 21st was also the first day of summer, the longest day of the year.

"Of course," Alicja answered, hesitant to look up.

"I've brought you a present. Please come sit here."

Reluctantly, she walked over to the beige couch where he sat in his pale blue lounging robe with his legs crossed. Beside him on the coffee table was a large box of raspberry-filled chocolates wrapped in burgundy paper with a gold bow. A single rose was taped to the top of the box. Franciszek placed his hand on Alicja's knee as she sat next to him. She felt her heart racing wildly.

"Open the box, my dear," he said softly. "This is not just any box of chocolate. I bought it at Krakow's finest shop. It's imported from Switzerland."

Alicja glanced at the elegantly wrapped box, aware that Franciszek was now moving his hand up and down her leg.

"I would like to teach you to appreciate the finer things in life," he continued. "I want to expose you to art and literature. I want to train your ears to listen to classical music—our beloved Chopin and others." He moved closer to her. "Come, Alicja, open the box."

"No, thank you, Papa," she heard her voice crackle and quickly got up. "I'm not very hungry right now."

The chocolate was still set on the coffee table when Genowefa came home from the doctor's office.

"Such a beautiful box of chocolate your father bought for you, Alicja. Don't you want it?"

"No, Mama, I don't."

"But it was very nice of him to bring it, wasn't it?"

"Yes, Mama. It was."

As grade school drew to a close, Alicja received yet another academic award. The familiar disparaging whispers following her in school that day stung like a whip.

"It's no surprise." "She thinks she's better than others." "Jews run the school, just like they run the world."

Franciszek was unmoved by Alicja's tears as she described the students' reaction to her award.

"Perhaps, Alicja, you do not always have to be best in the class and get so many awards. That way, you won't get so much attention, and you won't be made to cry."

Alicja looked at him quizzically, trying to hold back tears, trying to be strong. But the tears streamed out.

"But Papa . . ."

"And one more thing," he added, with a tone of finality that ended the encounter. "The next time you get an award I'm going to throw it out the window. We have enough problems around here already."

Having graduated from grade school, Alicja could pursue one of two educational options. The first was trade school. The second was *gymnazjum*, roughly the equivalent of American high school and early college. Poland's best and brightest came out of the gymnazjum programs, and gymnazjums competed among themselves for national honors. The Bochnia gymnazjum was among the best in the country. For Alicja, at the top of her grade school class, gymnazjum was the obvious choice.

Only Franciszek, who had withdrawn from her again, did not want her to go. Instead he urged her to go to trade school.

"Have a profession," he growled.

Alicja turned to Genowefa, and with her she found boundless support and loving companionship. Franciszek huffed his way back to work in Krakow.

Twenty-nine

May 2000
MACHU PICCHU, PERU

Lisa hoped a book she presented to Lucia would pique her interest and perhaps ease her anxious mind while she struggled in her "void." The book, *Anatomy of the Spirit*, was written by Caroline Myss, a pioneer in the fields of holistic health and medical intuition. Myss had since developed an interest in the language of symbols, myths, and archetypes.

Lucia was indeed drawn into the book, and she soon read the author's other works. They provided a meaningful context for her spiritual journey, and validated her own exploration of her symbolic dreams and visions.

In her books, Myss described three types of power: tribal, individual, and symbolic. Lucia identified "tribal" as those people and institutions who imposed rituals and expectations on its members, such as churches and synagogues. "Individual power" was what she was struggling towards. And the "symbolic power" Myss described represented to Lucia the highest power—the agent of change. Lucia believed that her visions and dreams, her inspired writings, and her deep meditations were all catalysts in her journey of change.

"I feel so much better now," she told Lisa after finishing

Anatomy of the Spirit. "Like I'm not so out-of-bounds with my life. Like I'm okay."

"You are more than okay," Lisa answered. "I'm sure you'll see that for yourself once we go to Machu Picchu. Caroline Myss is holding a seminar there."

"Where?" Lucia asked quizzically.

"Machu Picchu, in Peru."

Lisa handed Lucia an airplane ticket and an itinerary for the trip. Lucia was reluctant to take a long trip to a place she knew little about. Then a thought entered her mind: *another dimension.*

Nestled in a remote area of the Peruvian Andes, soaring above the Urubamba River, sits a sprawling, ancient landscape of agricultural and urban wonders known as Machu Picchu. Machu Picchu was a center of worship and astronomy, and a sanctuary for the preparation of priestesses and brides for the Incas, who originally inhabited the site beginning in the thirteenth century.

Lucia, Lisa, and a group of about three hundred people listened to Caroline Myss talk about the mind's powerful effects on physical and mental well-being. Lucia and Lisa felt over-whelmed by the size of the group, so Lisa arranged for them to take a semiprivate tour of Machu Picchu the next day.

"You must go early to see the amazing sunrise," a slim, weathered Peruvian tour guide told them.

So, well before dawn, Lucia, Lisa, and three other people joined the guide on the Cusco Railway that dropped them at the base of the Inca Trail. There they took a bus up to the trail that led to the Inca ruins. Their reward for the early start was a trail blissfully free of the crowds that would arrive later.

"From this point," the guide said, "there are only footpaths to the ruins."

He gave Lucia and another woman each a walking cane

for the ascent. Lucia examined her unusual cane, which had a pronounced, curved handle in what looked like the shape of a snake head. Its two eyes, carved into the wood, seemed to peer back at her.

"Alright everyone, let's go!" called the guide.

Lucia planted the cane in the ground, feeling a strange energy from the handle, and followed the small group to a clearing in the path.

"To the left," the guide announced, "are some of the Inca worship ruins. You'll be able to see them better when the sun rises in a little while. And to the right is a spot the Incas considered to be one the most intense centers of spiritual energy."

Lucia instinctively drifted to the right. A middle-aged man from New York named Jeffrey joined Lucia and Lisa. The three of them stood next to a small stone structure with a pedestal, no more than two feet high, at its center. Lisa and Jeffrey walked around the perimeter of the area while Lucia turned eastward, leaned against the structure wall, and waited. She basked in the rising sun, contemplating the energy she was feeling at this moment.

"Mother, come here—quick!" Lisa exclaimed.

Lucia rushed to join Lisa and Jeffrey.

"Look at this!"

They stood on a perch overlooking the valley, the sun reflecting magnificently on the rippling currents of the Urubamba River far below.

"Look straight ahead," Lisa directed. "Do you see the rainbow?"

Lucia saw the residue of a rainbow fading into the contours of the green and brown landscape.

"I see it," Lucia replied.

"Too bad it's fading," Lisa said, disappointed.

Lisa and Jeffrey wandered off to explore the perimeter.

Lucia remained on the perch overlooking the valley. Just then a new rainbow, bright and vibrant, appeared before her. She stood entranced, gazing at its brilliant hues. Her spirit seemed to lift out of her body and she extended her arms forward. She felt as if she was flying under the arch of the rainbow, entering the gates of heaven.

"Lisa, Lisa! Look!"

Lisa and Jeffrey ran over. They couldn't believe what they saw—Lucia's figure, arms outstretched, silhouetted against the horizon, like a shadow on a concrete sidewalk, framed in a beautiful rainbow.

"Hurry, Lisa. Take a picture. No one will believe this."

Lisa fumbled through her knapsack, grabbed her camera, opened the lens and squinted through the viewfinder. But before she could press the shutter, the rainbow disappeared, and Lucia's silhouette with it.

"The rainbow was meant only for your mother," said Jeffrey.

Lucia and Lisa told the Peruvian guide what had happened later that morning.

"I'm stunned," he said. "Rainbows are common here, but I've never heard of anyone having an experience like that."

Another dimension, Lucia recalled.

More than two weeks after her trip to Machu Picchu, Lucia still could not settle into "normal" day-to-day life. She brought the strange cane home with her, arousing the curiosity of airport security. She was curious too, yet did not know what to do with the cane.

Her rainbow experience dominated her thoughts. A few years earlier, she recorded a dream in her journal of a skyscraper, like the Empire State Building, lit up like a rainbow in predominately violet light. Rainbows, she knew, symbolized a connection between heaven and earth and a sign of a covenant between God and mankind.

She felt she had somehow bridged heaven and earth in Machu Picchu. Yet what was she supposed to do *now*? Perhaps the bridge *did* reach into heaven. But what was expected of her back on earth?

Thirty

August 1954
BOCHNIA, POLAND

Admitted to the prestigious Bochnia gymnazjum, Alicja eagerly, if nervously, anticipated the start of school a few weeks away. She and Genowefa were organizing her school supplies one afternoon when someone knocked on their door. It was a woman in her forties wearing a sky blue dress and a string of milky white pearls, clearly a woman of means.

"My name is Pani Zlowaska," the woman said. "My daughter, Marysia, will be entering the same class as Alicja."

Genowefa invited her in. Alicja was instantly enamored with the woman. She noticed her looking around at the dingy walls, the old furniture, and the worn and torn couch, and worried that she might also see the straw bed that she slept on. Alicja suddenly felt ashamed of how they lived.

Genowefa and Pani Zlowaska sat at the kitchen table. Genowefa offered the woman a cup of tea and a cherry danish, which Pani Zlowaska happily accepted.

"I would very much like it if Alicja could become Marysia's friend," Pani Zlowaska said.

It occurred to Genowefa that Alicja had grown up without any close friends, and she felt a wave of sadness.

"Oh my, I almost forgot. I have something for you, my dear." Pani Zlowoska directed her attention to Alicja. She reached into her purse, took out a small wrapped box and handed it to Alicja. "Go ahead, open it. I bought one just like it for Marysia." It was a journal for school, the nicest Alicja had ever seen. She stroked the purple-felt cover, a broad smile brightening her face.

"It's beautiful. Thank you." Alicja ran to the couch to curl up with her gift. She wanted to write what she was thinking. Why would such a wealthy woman want her daughter to be friends with a Jewish girl from a poor house? But her pen did not move. She listened to the conversation between Genowefa and Pani Zlowoska.

"Marysia tells me Alicja was the best student in the school," Pani Zlowoska exclaimed. "And I've also heard that she's a very devoted daughter and churchgoer. She's the kind of girl I want my Marysia to be around."

Alicja wanted to let out a resounding, joyous roar. Her years of effort and struggle had been validated. She wanted to go onto the balcony, where cracks from the shattered brick were still visible, stretch out her hands, and shout a proclamation of victory.

Alicja and Marysia became fast friends, studying together, listening to music, and leafing through teen magazines. Marysia was a head taller than Alicja, her long, curly black hair accenting her stature even more. She wore clothes bought in Krakow's finest stores. Yet they walked through the halls of the gymnazjum together like sisters, as if there were no differences between them.

Alicja was certain, though, that Marysia would abandon the friendship once she encountered her landlord, Chmielewski. The two girls had always met at Marysia's home, but one day Marysia insisted on visiting Alicja at the Swiateks' house. Alicja was reluctant but finally consented to allow Marysia to accompany her home one day after school. Chmielewski still cursed and sometimes threatened Alicja when he saw her. She never knew what to expect when she passed through the alley by his door. So when she and Marysia entered the alley, Alicja took her friend's hand, held it firmly, and pulled Marysia quickly past Chmielewski's door. Thankfully, on this day there was no incident.

Alicja continued to maintain high academic standards, earning respect and admiration from the school headmaster and director, Albert Bernacki. His gentle soul and deep, calm baritone voice soothed Alicja at every assembly introduction.

Recognizing Alicja's gifts, Bernacki tapped her for leadership positions in student government. He asked her to present the current events program to the student assembly. There she gave a presentation on a matter that concerned all of Poland, if not Europe. In part it read:

> My fellow students: Today, I must report that the safety and security of our country is in peril. A number of treaties were signed in Paris on October 23rd. West Germany has been accepted into the North Atlantic Treaty Organization, an organization of aggressive Western powers. How does this affect us? West Germany will be allowed to have weapons again. I don't think I need to tell anyone what seeing Germans with weapons means to us. I am hopeful that Chairman Bierut will enlist the support of Chairman Khrushchev and our Soviet allies to protect our western boundaries.

Alicia's presentation drew much applause from the student body. Bernacki was visibly proud. He felt that a bright future lay ahead of her.

Thirty-one

February–August 2001
NEW YORK, NY

Lucia welcomed a second grandchild in February 2001. Mitchell and Beverly named him Joshua, after the biblical warrior and prophet tasked with carrying on Moses's legacy in a new land. Lucia appreciated this, yet she also believed that there was additional symbolic meaning to his being named Joshua, one that she was not yet prepared to reveal.

To honor his father, Mitchell also gave his son his father's Hebrew name, Chanoch. At the boy's *bris*, the circumcision ceremony, Mitchell spoke about how Herman had carried on the European traditions of his family despite the loss of his family and home in the war.

More than a year after her adventure in Machu Picchu, Lucia felt her spiritual sensibilities heightened. But a key question remained: what did the heavens expect of her on earth?

In late August 2001, this question took on unexpected weight. On the night of August 23, she had two powerful dreams which she recorded in her journal. The first dream entry reads:

I am inside a tall glass building and see dark clouds overhead.

*Strong winds push debris from airplanes around the building. I
see people jumping from windows. I am safe, though, like I am in
a protective bubble.*

The second dream entry reads:

*I am in a meeting hall, or a home, and hear noise from a party
taking place below me. I find a stairwell and begin to walk down
the steps. But the stairwell ends suddenly and there is a large gap
between the end of the stairwell and the lower level floor where the
party is being held. A presence carries me across the gap and sets
me down on the floor of the lower level.*

*I am then called to a stage at the front of the room. A huge clock
with Hebrew letters is perched on the stage. I am asked to move the
arm of the clock, but I don't know where I am supposed to move
it. I hear "move the [Hebrew] letter* shin.*" Then I feel a presence
taking hold of my hand, this time moving it to adjust the clock to
the three o'clock position. When I complete my task, I hear loud
applause from the crowd. I sit down at a table set with an array of
pastries and wine. My grandson, Joshua, is there too. The crowd
begins to chant the* Birchat Hamazon, *the Grace after Meals.*

While recording the first dream, Lucia recalled an earlier
vision where she was in a protective bubble as a tornado raged
past. Both dreams seemed to indicate that she was being pro-
tected in the storms and chaos of her life. But the second dream
with the huge clock, the Hebrew letter *shin,* and the number 3
was baffling. Its symbolism seemed significant, but she couldn't
decipher it. Although several blank pages remained in her journal,
she placed it in her safe. Later she bought a new journal for
September, a month she hoped would provide fresh answers.

Thirty-two

April 1955
BOCHNIA, POLAND

Alicja and Marysia walked side by side with the first year gymnazjum class as they made their way to the school chapel. The transition from classroom to chapel was always a noisy one, with students eager to let loose after a morning of studies. But the priest, leading the students, made clear his insistence on dignity and reverence.

By the time he passed under the large crucifix adorning the entrance not a whisper disturbed the silence. The priest distributed a pamphlet entitled *Recolekcje,* a guide for the Easter Passion service he was about to lead.

The priest began: "We adore you, O' Christ, and we praise you." The students repeated this in unison, bowing their heads.

Alicja bowed her head as well, just as she had done many times before at St. Mikolaj. But this was the first time that Alicja recalled attending an Easter service without her mother.

The priest continued to read. "The Jews did not heed Jesus. They mocked him and ridiculed him."

Alicja noticed some of her classmates turning to look at her. Her eyes met the gaze of one of the girls and she quickly looked away. She'd heard priests at St. Mikolaj say those words before, but no one there had ever turned to look at her *that* way.

Now Alicja's chest tightened as the priest continued to read.

"Consider how Jesus, in making this journey, did so thinking of us, and for us offered to his Father the death he was about to undergo."

At each Passion "station," as Jesus's suffering intensified, so did the glares some of her classmates directed at her.

"Pilate offered to release Jesus, but the Jewish priests and elders clamored for his crucifixion."

She felt dizzy, at one point leaning into Marysia, who took Alicja's hand and held it firmly.

"Alicja, you don't look very well," Marysia whispered. "Perhaps I should walk you to the nurse." Alicja nodded.

At the nurse's office on the first floor of the school, Marysia asked whether Alicja could be excused for the rest of the day. The nurse consented and escorted Alicja to the exit.

"Thank you, Marysia," Alicja muttered before leaving the school building.

Alicja walked along the familiar street towards home. She decided to stop at the old cemetery she'd been visiting since grade school. There, with the cold wind scattering leaves over the graves and squirrels scampering on the ground, she tried to order her thoughts.

She knew her Jewishness made her different from everyone else in town. She'd been teased, cursed at, and even threatened because of it. Sometimes she heard people saying bad things about Jews. But other than the men she saw from the Jewish agency when she was a little girl, and the few moments she barely remembered spending with the relative who'd burst into their home wanting to send her to a Jewish orphanage, she had never known anyone Jewish. She thought that the teases and curses she had to endure were because of how people remembered the way Jews must have acted.

But what had happened this day in the school church was unlike anything she'd experienced before. It wasn't just about her being different, or about the ill feelings people in town harbored toward the Jews who once lived among them. It now seemed that the source of their animosity reached all the way back to the Passion. Was that why her landlord hated her so much? Was that why so many Jews—including her parents—were killed?

Alicja's mind raced as disturbing questions arose. Did the glaring students think she was personally responsible for what happened to Jesus? Was *she* responsible? If so, why had she been spared while her parents died?

Alicja walked through the cemetery, letting the questions settle. Then a curious thought entered her mind. Perhaps there was a reason she had survived. Perhaps she had been chosen to survive in order to repent and pray for the Jewish people.

Yet as she considered this possibility, a perplexing new question arose. How would she pray? As a Catholic? As a Jew? *"What am I?"* she asked herself. She had never considered this question before. And standing in the cemetery, silent but for the stirring of the spring breeze, she realized she didn't know the answer. And not knowing this, she wondered if she should pray at all.

When she returned home she told her parents what had happened at the service. For once, Franciszek was sympathetic.

"Jesus would be appalled at what the church has done in his name," he said. "Jesus was himself a Jew. He loved his own people."

"Jesus was Jewish?"

"Of course he was. Everyone knows this."

Alicja was astonished. She had not known this. She'd never heard it mentioned before. Now nothing made sense.

When Alicja returned to school the next day, she sat several rows behind her usual seat in her classrooms. And while she still completed her school work diligently, typically in advance of due dates, she was not the first to raise her hand during class discussions. And in the post-Easter school church services, she continued to seek out God's love and Jesus's protection, but she did not chant any prayers in unison with her classmates.

By the end of her first year at the gymnazjum, Alicja received an outstanding achievement award and a scholarship to an exclusive summer camp in the Carpathian Mountains. She quickly placed the certificate in her backpack, hoping that her classmates would not find out about it. That was the last thing in the world she needed.

PART THREE

Thirty-three

September 2001
NEW YORK, NY

On Tuesday, September 11th– the morning that shocked the world—Lucia sat stunned, as did so many watching the horrific events unfolding on the television screen. Living on the Upper West Side of Manhattan, she called Lisa, working in Midtown, and Mitchell, in Rockville, Maryland, and was relieved that they were okay.

But Lucia wasn't certain that *she* was okay. The television endlessly replayed the flight of the airplanes into the Twin Towers. She looked out the window of her sixth floor apartment; the streets below were eerily quiet. She recalled her dream of a calamity in a tall glass building filled with airplane debris and people jumping out of the windows. Could she have done something? Should she have warned someone? Was taking some preemptive action what the heavens had expected from her?

But what *could* she have done? Stand on a street corner warning passersby of an approaching catastrophe like some urban prophet? Surely her dreams and visions didn't require that. People would think she was mad.

I am not a prophet, she told herself.

Everything that had happened to her since her trip to Tyrol with Herman, all her mystical or prescient dreams and experiences, were part of a *personal* journey. She was learning about herself. That was all. She was not responsible for world events. Still, her dream of a calamity in a tall glass building haunted her.

Then there was the matter of the other dream she'd had on the same night—the one with the huge clock, the Hebrew letter *shin,* and the number 3. That dream now required further exploration.

In the following weeks, Lucia immersed herself in books on the Kabbalah, talked to rabbis, and listened to cassette tapes investigating the letter *shin.* She learned that Hebrew words and letters often contain multiple interpretive meanings, and that each Hebrew letter also carries a numerical value that, in Kabbalistic tradition, can have one or more mystical meanings.

From several sources she learned that the letter *shin*:

• Represents a balancing energy of good and evil;
• Symbolizes a bridge between the worlds of physical and metaphysical existence;
• Contains healing energy;
• Is the first letter of two of God's names—*Shaddai* (Almighty) and *Shalom* (Peace).

Lucia also learned that in Kabbalistic tradition, *shin* is assigned a numeric value of 300. And in a book on numerology she learned that multiple digits can be reduced through addition to a single digit. Thus 3 + 0 + 0 = 3. So the letter *shin* could also represent the number 3. She was seeking the relevance of her dream, in which a voice had told her to "move the letter *shin*," and a presence then guided her to move the hands on the clock to the three o'clock position. Still, the meaning of this symbolism eluded her.

She shared these thoughts with Mitchell, who had supported

her throughout her journey. He had his own mystical experiences, often in synchronicity with hers, yet he was skeptical now.

"You were told to move the clock to the three position?" he asked. "That's the letter *gimmel,* not *shin.* The letter *gimmel* corresponds to the number three. There is no *shin* on a Hebrew clock."

"I can't pretend to explain it," she said. "I only know that it was not a mistake. Nothing I have experienced is false. There is only meaning I do not yet understand."

Mitchell acknowledged this.

"I guess sometimes meaning has to unfold in its own time," he said.

Thirty-four

June 1959
BOCHNIA, POLAND

Over the next few years Alicja continued to excel in her gymnazjum studies. As her final year progressed it was clear to all that she would be graduating with honors. Director Bernacki supported her plans to attend university to study biology.

But her plans unexpectedly changed midyear when Genowefa suffered a heart attack and had to stop her dressmaking work. Up until now, Genowefa had been supplementing the salary Franciszek brought home. In fact, Franciszek had only been bringing home half his earnings. The other half remained in Krakow, where Franciszek kept a mistress.

It was an arrangement Genowefa reluctantly lived with. At one time, when Alicja was still in grade school, Genowefa had taken a train to Krakow and confronted Franciszek's mistress, begging her to not break up their family. "What family?" the young woman responded. "Francisek told me that a Jewish girl was living in your home." Genowefa did not relent, seeking out the woman's parents and confronting them. That ended the relationship but Franciszek punished her with a beating and a threat of divorce. Genowefa yielded, and a subsequent mistress followed.

Now, with Genowefa no longer able to work and bring home supplemental income, Alicia could not afford to go to university. She'd have to go to work instead. It was a crushing blow. She wished that Genowefa had not told her about the confrontation with the former mistress. She wished she did not know that Franciszek was keeping half his income to himself. And she didn't want to think about the mistresses he had acquired since that time. She'd worked so hard in school. Her friend Marysia was planning to enroll in the same program that she wanted to pursue.

Now she'd have to look for a job instead. She had no idea what kind of job she could get with a liberal arts education from gymazjum. Reluctantly, she turned to Franciszek for help.

"I don't know what to tell you," Franciszek snapped. "You should have gone to trade school like I told you to."

"But Papa—"

"But nothing. You didn't listen. Now look what position you're in."

Alicja had hoped that by now Franciszek would have put her rejection of his advances behind him. Apparently he had not. He refused to help her.

She eventually found a job as a cashier behind a thick glass window at a train station in Brzesko, dispensing tickets for travelers to Krakow and other destinations. She wore her hair pulled back in accordance with work regulations, and her wool, navy blue uniform itched uncomfortably. But she was bringing a paycheck back to Genowefa. Hers was a small sacrifice compared to Genowefa's sacrifices for her for so many years.

Alicja became familiar with the mostly male faces of the morning commuters. One man, tall and broad-shouldered with thick black hair, began to take a few moments longer to count his change at her booth after purchasing his ticket. She felt herself blush whenever he came by.

One evening near the end of her shift, as she sat in her booth engrossed in a magazine, she heard a tapping on the glass. She looked up and she saw the black-haired man. For an instant she thought she was back at her morning shift.

"I see you every morning and I don't even know your name," the man said.

"A-Alicja," she said softly, feeling awkward in his presence.

"I am Stephan. I've actually wanted to ask you something for awhile now."

Alicja braced herself; she wasn't sure what she was bracing for.

"Oh, what did you want to ask?"

She reached nervously for her ticket roll and accidentally dropped it on the floor. She bent down to pick it up. Stephan waited for her face to reappear in the window, a nervous smile on his face.

"If you would be so kind, may I ask for the pleasure of your company for a walk in the park tomorrow evening?"

Alicja sat in stunned silence, apparently long enough to cause Stephan to turn aside and begin plotting his way out of this uncomfortable encounter.

"Yes," Alicja heard herself say. "I guess—yes."

Stephan was at the train station the next morning as usual, but this time he winked at Alicja after he had purchased his ticket and told her he'd see her tomorrow. Alicja was momentarily confused; were they not they meeting today after work? She studied his expression, quickly concluded that he was joking, and returned his playful smile. Time passed painfully slowly as the day progressed. On at least two occasions a customer had to tap on the glass to draw her attention away from the pocket mirror she held to ensure that her hair and make-up were pristine. Finally she saw Stephan approaching the ticket booth. She wondered if she was ready. Did her hair need one more brush-through? Was her lipstick fading? Too late. He was at the booth.

Stephan seemed to sense her nervousness and warmly extended his hand. Alicja placed her hand in his, feeling a rush of sensation she'd never felt before. They walked to the park, only ten minutes from the train station. The leaves on the trees were vibrant shades of burgundy, orange, and yellow in the late October autumn air. Then they walked to the town square, where Stephan had made dinner reservations at an elegant café. The conversation seemed effortless. Stephan talked about his journey into law and his work as a practicing family lawyer. Alicja shared her plans to attend university. The train station attendant job was a just a brief diversion, she told Stephan. He'd never been to Bochnia, but he'd heard it was a nice town. Both of them, though, loved Krakow. Stephan said that the next time they went out he would take her to Krakow.

Before long Stephan was regularly taking Alicja to Krakow from Brzesko, a trip that took over an hour by train. They attended concerts and dined in cafés along the perimeter of Krakow's glorious main market square, one of the oldest and largest in all of Europe. They strolled through the Sukiennice, the centerpiece of the town square, a Renaissance-era marketplace bustling with vendors of clothes, crafts, and exotic imports.

Winter arrived, and Stephan took Alicja to Krakow during the first snow of the season. They played in the town square like schoolchildren, throwing snowballs at each other. At one point Stephan ran into a narrow cobblestone alley off the main square. Alicja chased after him, but found the alleyway deserted. She stopped, wondering where he could be. Suddenly a scarf was placed over her face. She turned around with a start, and there he was. "Stephan!"

He laughed uproariously. Then he gently drew her close to

him, placed his snow-moistened lips on hers, and they kissed. Long after they parted, Alicja could still feel the warmth of his embrace and the tenderness of his lips. Could this be love, she wondered? She would talk to Marysia about it. But she felt like she was falling in love with Stephan.

By mid-December the sights and scents and lights of Christmas began illuminating Krakow and other Polish cities. Stephan offered to visit Alicja in Bochnia to help with the decorations. After some hesitatiton, Alicja agreed. She thought that Stephan ought to meet Genowefa and perhaps Franciszek as well.

Both Franciszek and Genowefa were charmed by Stephan. Like Franciszek, Stephan had a keen interest in classical Greek philosophy. And Genewefa discovered that Stephan's family was friendly with a distant cousin of hers living in Brzesko. Franciscek seemed especially animated after the visit.

"Nineteen is not too young to get married," he remarked.

Alicja glared at Franciszek and turned away. She wasn't ready for marriage, though she cherished a girlish notion of finding a prince who would be devoted to her for all time. It was enough for now to be in love with Stephan, and to believe that he was in love with her. And she did not want Franciszek involved with any of this.

"I'm so happy for you, moya swotka," Genowefa beamed. "What a lovely young man. You deserve happiness. No one deserves it more."

The next day, Genowefa eagerly contacted her cousin in Brzesko. "You must tell Stephan's mother what a wonderful girl he is seeing."

"I will," Genowefa's cousin said. "And all the best to you and Franciszek."

Stephan was at the train station, as usual, the next workday morning. Alicja anticipated chatting about his visit to Bochnia and looked forward to discussing their plans for the evening. But Stephan had a strange look on his face, and his eyes avoided hers. He handed her his ticket money standing sideways, his arm extended outward. His manner was so distant that Alicja didn't know what to say. She looked at him, baffled, said nothing, and slid his ticket and change through the window. He took them and walked away without looking at her.

She spent the rest of the day trying to figure out his strange behavior. Maybe she was too young and awkward for him. Maybe she had failed to please him. Maybe he needed a more mature woman. In any case, he had made himself clear: the courtship was over. Alicja was devastated.

At dinner that evening Genowefa told Alicja about her conversation with her cousin in Brzesko. Her cousin had apparently told Stephan's mother that Alicja was Jewish. And now Stephan would have nothing to do with her.

Alicja burst into tears. She was the same girl Stephan had seemed to be in love with only a few days ago. There was nothing Jewish about her other than her birth. She knew nothing of Jewish rituals, beliefs, or observances. In fact, she was a more devoted churchgoer than he was. Yet to Bochnia, to Stephan, and, she supposed, to all of Poland, she was and always would be a Jewish girl, different than others.

Thirty-five

November 2001
NEW YORK, NY

I *hear "move the [Hebrew] letter shin." Then I feel a presence taking hold of my hand, this time moving it to adjust the clock to the three o'clock position.*

Lucia scoured through her old journals, searching for dreams she'd had where numbers figured prominently. She found several. In the fall of 2000, over the Yom Kippur holiday, she dreamed that she was walking on a street that split into two lanes. One lane was marked with the number 10 and the other with the number 9. She chose to proceed along the number 9 lane. Later that same year, she dreamed that she was at a train station. She looked at the clock prominently displayed above the train schedules and noted that it was twelve o'clock sharp.

She placed a clean sheet of paper on her desk and wrote down the numbers featured in her dreams:

9   12   3

Now what? she wondered.

She opened her journal and was inspired to write this:

Create a clock with the numbers and connect them, creating a tri-angle.

Create a clock? Connect the numbers to form a triangle? How

was she going to do that? She tenuously gripped her pen and drew a circle on the next page of her journal. Then she placed the numbers 9, 12, and 3 as they would appear on the face of a clock. Next she placed a dot in the middle of the circle to represent the gear mechanism that supports the hour, minute, and second hands. Now it was clearer as to how she could connect the numbers to form a triangle. She held her pen more firmly and drew a straight line connecting the numbers. When she was finished, she gazed at what she had drawn. It was just a circle with some numbers connected by a triangle and a dot on the inside. But what did it mean?

She glanced at the strange drawing for a few moments and was then inspired to write more:

Add 9 +12 + 3 and you will know where you are on your journey.

Like her dream of the *shin* on the clock, she thought that there was meaning beyond the immediate direction. But what did add-

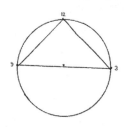

ing numbers have to do with her journey? She released her pen and contemplated closing the journal and going out for a break. But she couldn't move. She'd made a choice to follow this path. And this was a moment to fully immerse herself in the process. Her mind raced now. She recalled from her Kabbalah studies that multiple digits could be reduced through separation and addition to a single digit, so that, for instance, the number 300 can be separated to read 3 + 0 + 0 and then added for a sum of 3. Thus, the 12 in the equation of 9 + 12 + 3 can be separated into 1 + 2 for a sum of 3. Now the equation can be read like so: 9 + 3 + 3 for a sum of 15. The number 15 can be further separated into 1 + 5 for a sum of 6.

She paused, as if she'd just sprinted on a track hurdling over a maze of numbers and formulas that reached up from the pavement.

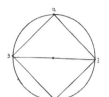

Lucia again turned to a fresh page in her journal and wrote down the numbers she was now working with:

9   12   3   6

It took a moment to realize what they were: *the four cardinal points on a clock!* She drew a circle underneath the numbers, placed them where they appeared on a clock, and connected them all with two triangles.

After pondering this she was inspired to write the following in her journal:

> *Where you go next on your journey depends on your will. You need to understand God's will and God's rules.*

She drew in a deep breath and tried to absorb the meaning of what she had written, words that were not her own. She reflected that her "will" on this journey was to find deeper meaning. Perhaps that deeper meaning was God's will.

Lucia was then inspired to interconnect the two triangles. To her surprise, she looked down at the paper and discovered that she had created a six-pointed star.

She had drawn the familiar figure, known as the Magen David (shield of David, or, as it is more commonly known, the Star of David). She sought to learn more about it. Clearly, it was the culmination of the Kabbalistic/numerology exercise she had just been through.

The Star of David is the symbol most commonly associated with Judaism today. Some suggest that it was the emblem on King David's shield. Historically, others have associated the Star or Shield of David with a representation of God's protection. The hexagram currently linked to the Star of David has been used by other religions as well, symbolizing the

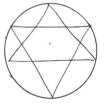

union of the masculine and feminine aspect of God or the union of heaven and earth, with God reaching down to man and man reaching up to God.

Lucia related her journey to many of these symbolic or mystical meanings. Yet when she returned to one of the sources that she had first consulted to understand the meaning of the letter shin, Kabbalist Rabbi Shraga (Philip) Berg's *The Energy of the Hebrew Letters*, she found an interpretation of the Star of David that is connected to King David and the Moshiach, or Messiah. It is said that the Messiah will be a descendant of the house of David. As such, the Star of David is more than merely decorative or symbolic. As Rabbi Berg notes, it is said to contain awesome power, a vital force of energy necessary to end war and suffering.

Now she understood that she still might not yet have a complete grasp of where her journey was going or what was expected of her, but it was clear that the dreams and writings that infused her spiritual work were not random or arbitrary incidents. They were part of a bigger plan.

Thirty-six

Winter-Spring 1960
BOCHNIA, POLAND

T he day after Stephan abruptly ended their relationship, Alicja quit her job at the Brzesko railway station. She hoped it would never come to this, but she saw no alternative to asking Franciszek for help once again.

He had rebuffed her request before, saying she should have gone to trade school. But when Stephan had visited their home just before Christmas, he seemed more accessible and amiable than he had been in years.

As director of finance with the Polish state railways, he was in a position to help. She did not want to look for another clerk position at a local train station. And the more she thought about it, Krakow would be a much better place for her to work than the stifling confines of Bochnia.

In Krakow, she could be anonymous, just another small town girl trying to make her way in the big city. So she waited for a moment when he seemed to be in a good mood. And then she asked for his help.

"A job in Krakow—with me?" he growled. "There's nothing I can do. You need training. You need a degree in finance, or at the very least a certificate in accounting." Alicja grimaced. She figured that could take months or years. But she saw no other options.

So, with money she saved from her job in Brzesko she enrolled in an accounting certificate program. It typically took one year to complete the program, but she completed it in six months. Now she could apply for a job with the railways. But obtaining a position was still difficult. There was bureaucracy and cronyism to deal with, and getting a job often came down to who you knew. Franciszek remained her best chance of being hired, but he'd already made it clear he didn't want to help her. Alicja was reluctant to approach him yet again.

"You must ask your father one more time," Genowefa told her. "Show him your certificate. He won't turn you away now."

Alicja took the train to Krakow and walked into the railway finance office. She approached the receptionist situated in the cavernous lobby and asked to speak with Franciszek Swiatek. The secretary placed the call, then informed Alicja that Franciszek was in a meeting now but would be out to meet her in a few minutes. Alicja paced the lobby, the heels of her shoes echoing off the polished hardwood floor.

Franciszek emerged about twenty minutes later. Alicja ran to him, holding the framed certificate in accounting in her hand.

"Look Papa," she said, and handed it to him.

Franciszek looked startled to see it. Then he glanced over it with a mixture of pride and exasperation.

"Now can you help me, Papa? I don't have to be in the same office as you," she tried to assure him. She couldn't care less about his mistress now. "I can work in another division, or in another building if you like. Can't you please help me?"

"Alicja, there's nothing I can do."

"Papa?"

Tears welled up in her eyes. Franciszek's exasperation turned to anger.

"I told you there's nothing I can do! You've sided with

your mother all these years—ask her for help!" He turned and walked away, disappearing into the corridor beyond the lobby. Alicja stood frozen for a few moments, and then forced herself to walk out of the building. She stopped and leaned against a column, just below the crest of the Polish republic, and cried for her life.

It had all come crashing down on her. Francisczek had refused to help. How could he do that to her? And Stephan had hurt her so—like a dagger to her heart. Now what was she supposed to do? She could not afford to attend university. She would never be able to find a decent job. And she would never be able to find love again—who would love a Jewish girl? She had come to a dead end. There was nowhere for her to go.

Alicja wept the entire return trip to Bochnia.

"What happened?" Genowefa asked, though she could already guess the cause of Alicja's tears.

She stroked Alicja's hair and pulled her close to her chest. It pained her to see Alicja hurt. She would do anything for her, but what could she do now? What could she say to Alicja to console her? She hated this feeling of helplessness and hopelessness. She pictured Franciszek slithering about his office, smugly making plans for the evening. How could he do this her? To Alicja?

Now Genowefa felt sweat dripping down from her arms. Her pulse raced. She released Alicja and stormed over to the kitchen counter. She grabbed a washcloth and began wiping the counter, the stove, and then the refrigerator. She wiped down the windowsills; she mopped the floor; she scrubbed dishes that had already been scrubbed.

"Mama, your heart, please slow down," Alicja pleaded with her.

But Genowefa could not slow down. She entered the bedroom and began wiping the dresser. In her rage, she shook the dresser violently. The drawers opened, the top one slipped off its hinges, and she saw the edge of a yellowed piece of notepaper, creased and lodged in the crack. She carefully pulled out the paper and unfolded it. It was a letter written in black ink, dated November 16, 1945. It read:

> *Dear Panni and Pan Swiatek,*
> *I believe you are caring for my niece, Adele's little girl. I somehow survived the horrible nightmare and am living in Bolivia. Can I be of any help to you? Adele was such a beautiful girl. Her daughter must be precious.*
> *Best wishes,*
> *Helen Blatt*

"Alicja!" Genowefa shrieked. "Alicja, come here right away! You won't believe what I've found."

Thirty-seven

May 2002
NEW YORK, NY

Where you go next on your journey depends on your will. You need to understand God's will and God's rules.

—From Lucia's journal

More than a year had passed since 9/11. Like many, Lucia still grappled with its aftermath. Looking back at what she'd written in her journals, at her recorded dreams and inspired writings, she was certain she'd exercised her personal will by choosing to continue the lonely, often murky spiritual path she was on. But how could she know or understand God's will? How could anyone? She pondered the question one night in early May as she recorded the following dream:

I see a large gold envelope near my bed. There is the most beautiful flame coming from it—a white and gold flame. But the envelope is not consumed by the flame.

The symbolism of the dream wasn't hard to decipher; it evoked the biblical account of Moses and the burning bush. Its profound implication of a message or communication from God left her feeling overwhelmed. She considered the dream with Mitchell in their next conversation.

"What should I do?" she asked him. "This is more than I can take."

"Perhaps instead of asking *if* God is communicating to you, you need to ask *what* God is communicating to you," Mitchell said.

Thirty-eight

September 1960
BOCHNIA, POLAND

Helen Blatt was the sister of Alicja's maternal grandfather. When Genowefa originally received the letter fifteen years earlier, she had immediately written back. Weeks later her letter was returned undelivered. She mailed another letter with the same result. Helen Blatt did not contact her again. And Genowefa stuck the letter in her drawer and forgot it.

Genowefa was shaken by its rediscovery, but Alicja was indifferent. She had no recollection of the letter and had never heard of Helen Blatt.

"What difference does it make now?" she asked Genowefa.

"Maybe there is something we can do," Genowefa countered. She suggested reaching out to the Jewish agency in Krakow. Perhaps they could locate Helen Blatt, or Alicia's other birth relatives.

Alicja was reluctant. She still recalled how the Jewish agency had tried to take her from the Swiateks as a child.

"Perhaps they can help you find a job," Genowefa suggested, "or help pay for university."

"Hmm," Alicja murmured. "Perhaps."

So they contacted the Jewish agency in Krakow requesting help. Agency representatives told Alicja they would help find her a job and arrange for her to receive a monthly stipend. They offered to put her in touch with a Jewish family in Krakow, the Lawaszes, who had known Alicja's maternal grandparents. Finally, they talked about the growing opportunity and prosperity young Jewish people were enjoying in Israel.

Alicja expressed her gratitude for the job and stipend, and accepted their offer of an introduction to the Lawaszes. Yet she wondered why there was no mention of help with a scholarship for university.

The Lawaszes invited Alicja to join them for dinner on the first night of Rosh Hashanah, the Jewish New Year. Alicja took the train to Krakow and walked to their home from the station. She had never heard of the Jewish New Year nor visited a Jewish family, and she approached their doorway with caution.

Her hosts, Isaac and Ruth Lawasz, greeted her warmly and led her into the dining room. Alicja was struck by the elegance of the table settings and by the sweet aroma that filled the room. Glazed carrots were warming in the oven and a tray with sliced apples and a dipping bowl of honey was set at the head of the table, next to Isaac. These, Isaac told Alicja, symbolized the hopes of all Jews for a sweet new year.

Alicja rose with the family as Isaac said a blessing over wine and raisin challah. The blessings, said in Hebrew, sounded strange and harsh. She was relieved when family resumed speaking in Polish.

Ruth Lawasz soon emerged from the kitchen with a tray of something called gefilte fish. A gefilte fish ball was placed on Alicja's plate, a sphere of the unknown. The Lawaszes were nearly done consuming the dish when Alicja sensed their gaze on her and her untouched plate. Tentatively lifting her fork, she stabbed the fish ball, broke off a small piece, and lifted it to her mouth. Feeling a wave of nausea, she excused herself from the table. She returned moments later from the bathroom with a nervous smile.

The remainder of dinner was more appetizing—roasted chicken, glazed carrots and green beans. The Lawaszes never mentioned Alicja's grandparents, whom they had known. And Alicja did not ask about them.

"Alicja, what are your plans, now?" Ruth asked in a caring tone.

"I would like to go to university," Alicja answered.

"Has the Jewish agency talked to you about Israel?"

"They might have mentioned it."

"And what do you think?"

Alicja recalled Chmielewski's rants from her childhood. He had told her to "go to Palestine" and she always thought of Palestine, now the State of Israel, as a place of banishment.

"For a young girl like you it would be a wonderful," Ruth continued.

"Excuse me," Alicja interrupted, glancing at her watch. "I must apologize. It's getting late and I have to catch the train back to Bochnia and check in on my mother."

"We understand. Of course. Would you please consider joining us at synagogue tomorrow morning for the Rosh Hashanah service?" Ruth asked.

Alicja paused. She was about to decline the invitation when, to her surprise, she said, "Yes."

Detail of Klimt's *Portrait of Adele Bloch-Bauer I*. After dreaming and writing about a gold dress that appears to be of great significance, Lucia was introduced to the painting in 2007. The connection between the painting and her journey was amplified several years later when she encountered a third-century Judean articraft that contains the same esoteric pattern as the twentieth-century painting. The articraft also evoked a mystical experience she had in Jerusalem where she was compelled to trace her finger in a similar esoteric pattern along the face of the Western Wall. (Courtesy of Neue Galerie New York/Art Resource, NY.)

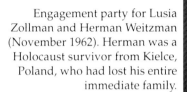

Engagement party for Lusia Zollman and Herman Weitzman (November 1962). Herman was a Holocaust survivor from Kielce, Poland, who had lost his entire immediate family.

Wedding of Lusia Zollman and Herman Weitzman. Herman, fourteen years older than her, changed the spelling of her name to Lucia—he deemed it more sophisticated.

Lucia, Herman, and young family. Lucia devoted herself to being a traditional Jewish wife and mother, raising two children in suburban Detroit. During this time, she suppressed the spiritual angst of her past in order to embrace a sense of belonging within the Jewish community.

Lucia, Herman, Mitchell, and Lisa in 1976. After many years in Detroit, Herman, never feeling rooted there and still scarred from the war years, takes the family out of Michigan. Years of declining health followed. He died in 1993, leaving Lucia a widow at age 53.

Lucia with Mitchell in 1994 at the Western Wall in Jerusalem, where a new phase of her life began.

Interior of Yemin Moshe Synagogue in Jerusalem. Note the painting of the golden eagle above the ark, which Lucia saw as a symbol of God's love and desire for unity.

Lucia and granddaughter Paula at Krakow's Tempel Synagogue celebrating Paula's Bat Mitzvah in 2011.

Lucia's grandchildren, Joshua Weitzman and Genna Edelstein.

Lucia with Marysia at the Bochnia Town Square in June, 1985, the first time she had visited her friend since she left Poland.

Lucia, Lisa, and another tourist at Machu Picchu, Peru (2000). Lucia holds
a cane given to her by a guide. The cane had a pronounced, curved handle
which looked like the shape of a snake's head. Its two eyes, carved into the
wood, seemed to peer back at her. The Moses-like reference was one of many
Lucia experienced throughout her journey.

Lucia at Macchu Picchu (2000). Lucia would later describe her experience there
as one of bridging heaven and earth. It emboldened her resolve to follow the
path she began at the Western Wall.

Lucia in Brzesko, Poland, her birth father's hometown (2004).

Lucia and Mitchell in Szebnie, Poland, in 2004, at the site where Lucia's father — and possibly her mother—died.

Jewish clay oil lamp, circa second–third century, c.e. (found in Jerusalem). Presented to Lucia by an Israeli archeologist in September 2012.

Less than a year later, on Mother's Day in 2013, Lucia returned to Neue Galerie to revisit Klimt's Portrait of Adele Bloch-Bauer. As she closely examined the painting, she made an extraordinary discovery. The esoteric design Klimt painted on Adele Bloch-Bauer's sleeve was the same design that appeared on her ancient Israeli lamp. It was also similar to a design she had felt Divinely inspired to trace on the stone blocks of the Western Wall. The convergence of these incidents hold deep symbolic meaning for her.

Thirty-nine

June 2002
RANCHO LA PUERTA, MEXICO

L ucia's dream of the golden envelope engulfed in flames that did not burn seemed like an escalation of her spiritual journey. But she felt like she needed human guidance: someone who could understand her experiences and not judge her, someone who could lead her beyond her library of mystical books. But where could she find such a person?

Lisa told her of a remarkable man, a progressive Jewish rabbi, who was presenting a seminar in Rancho La Puerta. Zalman Schachter-Shalomi, or Reb Zalman, as he was affectionately known, was born in Poland in 1924. After a traditional Orthodox upbringing he received rabbinic ordination from a Lubavitch Yeshiva in 1947. His career turned out to be anything but conventional: he actively engaged other religious and spiritual traditions and founded the Alliance for Jewish Renewal. He also wrote numerous books on prayer, Kabbalah, and spiritual growth.

Lucia signed up for the seminar, hoping Reb Zalman might understand and affirm her experiences, and perhaps offer direction. If only she could capture his attention for a few moments. She brought with her a journal in which she was capturing her dreams, visions, and inspired writings. One entry, her vision of the angel and the cloaked figure that evoked Jesus, particularly unnerved her. What would people think if they learned of this? What would her Orthodox relatives think? Even long after she was married and established her own home and family, her relatives remained an anchor in times of challenge and uncertainty. Her childhood fears of aloneness had never fully abated. She did not want to lose contact with her relatives any more than she'd wanted to leave the Swiateks. Yet if they learned about her dream vision of Jesus—a taboo subject to most Orthodox Jews— she didn't know what they'd do.

Perhaps she needed to simply forget the experience and remove it from her writings. Yet that too made her uneasy. She believed that the image of Jesus had appeared to her for a reason, though she was not certain why. And by now she was not inclined to dismiss any of her experiences, even if she did not fully understand them. She was in a quandary, and Reb Zalman seemed like the perfect person to help her resolve it.

At Rancho La Puerta, Reb Zalman was inundated with requests from admirers, colleagues and interviewers. But Lucia did catch the attention of Reb Zalman's wife, Eve Ilsen, in the resort's main lobby, and asked if she might speak briefly with the rabbi.

"What is it that you need from my husband?" Eve asked, tugging her curly silver hair.

Lucia presented her notebook. "I was hoping he could read this and talk to me about some questions I have."

"My husband has many demands on his time, but I'll see what I can do," Eve said, taking the notebook. "We'll talk again."

Lucia prepared herself for disappointment. Even if she did meet Reb Zalman, what would come of it? He'd probably think she was crazy.

At dawn the next morning, Lucia walked in the shadow of Mt. Kuchumaa, a sacred Indian mountain that dominates the Rancho site, and asked God: *why have I come here*?

She had brought along a new journal and was inspired to write:

Live every moment with the blessing the universe has bestowed upon you. Your prayer has been answered. There is nothing false in your writing. The reason for your being here is already established. I am that I am.

Lucia felt a shiver reading these words that were not her own. She walked back towards the hacienda, thinking to lie down in bed and meditate in her private room. As she approached the entrance she saw a note placed under her door.

Dear Lucia,
I was very touched by your story. My husband can see
you at 3pm.
Eve

Lucia walked to the main lobby at three o'clock and spotted Eve seated on a beige sofa just outside the lobby bar. Reb Zalman was seated next to her. She approached them cautiously, uncertain what to expect. Reb Zalman rose from the couch to greet her. He was wearing a black suit jacket over a white shirt, unbuttoned at the neck. He smiled warmly at Lucia, as if he'd seen her many times before. His grey beard and deep-set eyes accentuated an instant aura of piety, depth, and benevolence. Eve excused herself and Reb Zallman asked Lucia to take her place beside him.

"I've read what you wrote. It is an incredible journey you are on," Reb Zalman said. "What is it that I can do for you?"

Lucia relayed her concern about how her Orthodox relatives might react to her dream vision of Jesus.

She anticipated a long, thoughtful pause, but Reb Zalman responded immediately.

"I wouldn't worry about your relatives," he said. "Christians saved your life. Without them, there would have been no one to bring to America."

Lucia felt some relief with regard to her relatives, but she wasn't certain that Reb Zalman had fully addressed her internal conflicts.

"Spirituality comes from many religious traditions, Lucia. You must embrace that."

Lucia nodded. She *was* trying to embrace that. But all the rest of it—all the other mystical experiences—where was it all leading?

"What does all of this mean?" she asked him.

"I can't say," he replied. "This is, after all, *your* journey. But one thing is clear; much work still lies ahead of you. I can try to help when you need it."

Lucia decided she did need Reb Zalman's help. Several weeks later she and Lisa traveled to his hometown of Boulder, Colorado, where he and Eve were hosting a Jewish Renewal retreat.

"Your spiritual journey is unfolding nicely," he said, "but I don't know how much help I can offer. You need guidance on a regular basis. It's not enough to try to catch me here and there. Your journey deserves more. I think I know the right person to help you."

Reb Zalman told Lucia about a woman named Catherine Shainberg who lived in New York. Catherine Shainberg had a colorful background. She grew up in England and France, trained as an art historian at the School of the Louvre, moved to Israel, converted to Judaism, and spent ten years studying the Kabbalah with renowned Kabbalist and mystic Colette Aboulker-Muscat. She moved to New York in 1981, earned a doctorate in psychology, and wrote a book about Kabbalah and the power of dreaming.

Lucia returned to New York excited about the possibility of meeting this remarkable woman, but several calls to her went unreturned. When a woman finally answered the phone, identifying herself as Catherine's assistant, she indicated that Catherine was traveling a great deal as of late and she was not sure when she would be available.

Catherine's lack of availability felt like a setback. If there was much more work ahead of her, as Reb Zalman had suggested, how was she supposed to do it on her own? And how would she know if she was on the right track? If she once, in a dream vision, had been in a protective bubble as a tornado raged around her, she now felt exposed and vulnerable in a spiritual storm where lions, skyscrapers, Jesus, angels, rainbows, the letter *shin*, and a burning golden envelope whirled around her.

For the moment, she needed shelter from that storm. She put her journal away and took a long walk down Broadway, blending anonymously with fruit vendors, mothers with strollers, and harried businessmen flagging taxicabs headed downtown. She considered hailing a cab as well, only she wasn't sure where she wanted to go.

Forty

September 22, 1960
KRAKOW, POLAND

The next morning, before Genowefa and Franciszek awakened, Alicja caught an early train to Krakow and walked along the street clutching the scrap of paper with the address of the synagogue, 24 Ul. Miodowa, where she was to meet the Lawaszes. A cool breeze rippled through her white cotton blouse, prompting her to button up her navy blue blazer. She contemplated her impulsive acceptance of the Lawaszes' invitation to attend the Rosh Hashanah service.

On her many trips to Krakow, she'd never been to this section of town known as Kazimierz, at one time a thriving center of Jewish life. Faded Stars of David and Hebrew script marked dilapidated building entrances and abandoned store windows.

She finally reached 24 Ul. Miodowa and saw the words *Tempel Synagogue* inscribed above the entrance. Men in long black coats passed by her and entered, barely acknowledging her presence. A group of older women were gathered in front greeting each other warmly. Their familiarity with each other unnerved her. She thought of turning around, walking back to the train station and returning to Bochnia. But just then a man with a thick gray beard and soft brown eyes approached her.

Startled, she took a step back. The sight of him shook her unexpectedly. Then he began speaking to her in Yiddish.

"Nie rozumie," she said, meaning she did not understand.

The man placed his hand over his forehead.

"My dear," he said, "I am the rabbi here. Please come in. The ladies' section is through the door and up the stairs on the balcony."

He spoke in awkward Polish, clearly not his mother tongue. Alicja gazed at him. The rabbi radiated holiness—a Divine aura seemed to surround him. She instantly felt uncomfortable for thinking that. As a little girl sitting in the pews of St. Mikolaj she sometimes tried to envision what God looked like. This man, this rabbi, struck her as uncannily similar to those childhood conceptions.

The synagogue's interior was far more expansive than it appeared from outside. Though still in disrepair from Nazi destruction, its soaring ceilings and ornate décor retained a sense of its original 1862 design, patterned after the Leopoldstadter Tempel, the largest synagogue in Vienna.

Upon entering the women's section on the balcony, Alicja instantly noticed the chatter of the women drowning out the sounds of the service being conducted by the men below. She couldn't recall an instance where parishioners would talk to each other during Mass. Perhaps they were talking about her.

She was out of place, with no idea what to expect. What if she stood when she was supposed to sit, or sat when she supposed to stand? The rows were bunched so closely together—how was anybody supposed to kneel? She was sure her ignorance would quickly be exposed. Someone would find out that she was a churchgoer and swoop down at any moment and take her away. Or maybe Jewish agency representatives would recognize her after all these years and send her to Palestine. Her heart raced. A hand reached up and motioned for her to come over. It was Ruth Lawasz. Alicja cautiously made her way to Ruth, squeezing by two other women who Alicja sensed had been briefed about her arrival this morning. That's the one, she imagined them thinking. Ruth greeted her warmly and Alicja sat down beside her.

The service continued. She held on tightly to the prayer book that Ruth handed to her but didn't open it. None of the prayers would be familiar to her, just as the sanctuary, with its missing altar boys, crucifixes, and incense, was strange. She observed the men below. Some swayed wildly back and forth while others milled about the sanctuary. It seemed each was conducting his own service, only occasionally joining together in song. It was a disappointing spectacle, a far cry from the unified dignity of church. After less than an hour, Alicja got up from her seat, excused herself, and left. As she hurried toward the train station, she couldn't remember if she'd said good-bye to Ruth Lawasz.

After arriving at the Krakow train station for the forty-five minute ride to back to Bochnia, Alicja found a nearly empty car and sat alone, her thoughts racing.

Have I betrayed Mama? She cared for me, nurtured me, sacrificed for me, risked her life for me. Have I betrayed Jesus?

The train left the city limits and rolled through the countryside, past open fields, forests, and farmhouses. Alicja gazed out the window, listening to the rumble of the train, feeling a growing uncertainty. *Who was she? What was she? Christian or Jewish?*

She couldn't stop thinking about the rabbi she'd met outside the synagogue. She had felt something—what was it? A connection to her past? A spiritual presence? She didn't know. But the service was so chaotic, so foreign…how could they be her people?

The question surfaced again: *was she Christian or Jewish?*

She had the same uncertainty while wandering about the cemetery after the Easter Passion service during her first year at the gymnazjum. She didn't have an answer then, and she wasn't sure she had one now, six years later.

Maybe the Lawaszes were right when they talked about a better future for her in Israel. She could not hide her Jewishness in Poland. She was born Jewish; she could not escape that. Without the help of the Jewish agency, what kind of job could she get? And after Stephan cast her aside, she feared opening her heart to another man.

The night before at the Lawaszes' home, for the first time she had touched the pulse of Jewish life. Might she have a place in it? The rabbi had made her feel like she always belonged. The synagogue service was strange, but perhaps she'd get used to it.

A woman boarded the train at the next station stop and sat across from Alicja. A large gold cross hung from her necklace in stunning contrast to her jet black dress. The sight of the cross jarred her, and she awoke from her daydream. What was she thinking? Suddenly she was supposed to really be Jewish, not just be Jewish by birth? What about church? What about sharing Christmas with Genowefa? And what about Jesus, who'd given her strength and love for as long as she could remember?

She felt the impossibility of her circumstance. She was stuck in limbo between two worlds, acceptable to neither. As a Jew she was tainted to Christians. Yet as someone who clung to church and Jesus, wouldn't she be tainted to Jews?

Something had to be done to resolve her dilemma. All the doors in Poland were closed to her. Was it coincidence that just now another door was opening, that she felt pulled towards her heritage and a better future? She believed that a fateful decision had to be made, and made now. She loved Jesus and cherished the support her relationship with him had always brought her. But she could not get off the train with him. So, at the Bochnia station, she stepped from the train alone. The pain of her choice ripped her heart and tore the fabric of her spirit.

She waited for the other passengers to leave the station. Then she sat on a wooden bench and began to cry. Finally she stood and started walking home. Before entering she dried her tears.

Genowefa was in the kitchen wearing a worried expression. She wondered where Alicja had been all morning. Alicja went to her and held her tightly.

"I'm sorry, Mama," Alicja said, sinking her head in Genowefa's chest. "I was in Krakow and didn't realize how late it was. Please forgive me, Mama. Please forgive me."

Forty-one

August 2003
WASHINGTON, D.C.

For over a year Lucia felt her journey had stalled. She hadn't found a guide like Reb Zalman. She grew restless, waiting for something to happen. Then a friend asked Lucia to accompany her to the International Conference of Child Survivors and Their Families in Washington, D.C.

Lucia had long avoided attending Holocaust survivor conferences. Most survivors were much older than her, and their shared experiences of concentration and labor camps were not something she could relate to. Now a "next generation" of conferences for so-called hidden children like herself who had gone underground during the war, often in disguised identities to hide from the Nazis, were increasingly being offered.

Lucia began to consider the idea. She would be in the company of a small group of men and women who, as children, had somehow survived the odds and escaped the tragic fate of their Jewish family members, friends, and communities. Many of them, like her, had been raised by Christians who kept their Jewish identities secret. Many, like her, had been given new Christian names, identities and lives. Many, like her, were the only surviving members of their families. Attending the conference would be an opportunity to explore and emerge from the isolation of her past, to take measure of her life, and see how far she had come on her spiritual journey.

A natural curiosity took hold of her. How had her path compared with that of others? In the end she decided to attend the conference.

Over five hundred "hidden children," now grown, came from the United States, Latin America, Europe, Israel, and other places to attend the conference. After a keynote address, the conference broke off into various workshops. Lucia lingered outside a meeting room marked by a placard that read, "The Emotional Aftermath of the War Years." A stout woman in a burgundy dress gently wrapped her arm around Lucia and escorted her in. About twenty people were settling into two rows of chairs in a semicircle facing the facilitator. Lucia sat near one end of the back row. She planned to do a lot of listening, and no talking.

As the workshop progressed, people began to tell their stories. One woman told how she was hidden by monks in a monastery and reclaimed by her parents after the war. Though her parents survived, she nevertheless experienced a profound sense of abandonment. Another woman hidden in infancy by a gentile family didn't discover her Jewish identity until she was a teenager. She'd spent the better part of her life resenting the deceit.

Lucia found the stories compelling. But they were not *her* stories. And no one talked much about their current spiritual lives. She decided to leave the workshop when the next person started speaking.

"Lucia, tell us about yourself," the facilitator said, startling her.

"Me? There is not much to tell."

"I'm sure there is. This is a safe place for you to open up."

Lucia saw the other participants nodding.

"Really, there is not much to tell. I had a happy childhood. My parents who adopted me loved me."

"How long did you stay?" one woman asked.

"Did you go to church with them?" asked another.

"Sure. That was the only life my parents knew how to live."

"They didn't *force* you to go to church?" the second woman persisted.

Lucia's patience was running thin.

"No. Of course not. As I said, I had a wonderful childhood. Everything was perfect."

"How did you adapt to Judaism?" one of the men asked thoughtfully.

Lucia gave her pat answer.

"I always felt close to God, not to any particular religion." She hoped this would terminate the group interrogation.

As the workshop dispersed, one of the participants, a soft-spoken woman Lucia had hardly noticed, approached her.

"Tell me, Lucia," the woman began, "if everything was so perfect at home, why did you leave?"

The question cut Lucia to the quick. The truth about her life suddenly penetrated the story she had been telling herself all these years. She realized she hadn't been honest with the group, with her children, and, most of all, with herself.

Forty-two

October 1960 - Winter 1961
BOCHNIA, POLAND

The Jewish agency in Krakow had initiated a search for Alicja's possible relatives across Europe, Israel, and the United States. A woman named Sarah Barterer, a sister of Alicja's maternal grandfather, Josef Zollman, responded. Sarah and her husband had moved to Palestine before the war and now had a large family in the young State of Israel.

Sarah sent Alicja a letter of introduction and invited her to visit them in the Tel Aviv suburb of Petach Tikva. Inside the envelope was a photograph of a young girl. She was beautiful, playfully posing, with dark vibrant eyes and a flower in her short black hair. Then she noticed the writing on the back of the photo.

Adele Zollman, Age 16.

Alicja could hardly believe her eyes. Her hands trembled, holding for the first time a photograph of her mother. Her mother — a flesh and blood girl!

Alicja's thoughts spun at the enormity of this small photograph. What did it mean for her? What would it mean for Genowefa? She placed the photo in her purse and held it close to her chest.

The next letter from Sarah contained another invitation for Alicja to come to Israel. With money coming in from the Jewish agency, Alicja thought it would be best to delay rather than reject her acceptance of the invitation.

"I'm still thinking about it," she replied.

Sarah wrote again mentioning more of Alicja's relatives, first cousins to Josef Zollman, who lived in Long Beach, New York. One of them was Shoshana Twersky.

Shoshana contacted Alicja, recalling Adele as an adorable little girl everyone called Puppa (Doll). Shoshana's letter included photos of her large family: four handsome sons, their elegant wives, and beautiful children. Alicja was awed and strongly attracted to Shoshana's family.

Shoshana next wrote that she'd be sending Alicja some additional money to ease life for her and for the Swiateks. She gave Alicja instructions to meet a man in Krakow who would give her the money.

Alicja went to the address Shoshana had given her. A thin middle-aged man answered the door. After inquiring who she was, he invited her in and quickly handed her an envelope. The man did not introduce himself or say anything else to Alicja, who thought it better to not ask any questions. She knew that anything involving American money was taboo in communist Poland.

A month later, Shoshana again wrote to Alicja that money was being sent to her, with instructions to pick it up at the same address.

With the Jewish agency stipend and money coming from Shoshana Twersky, Alicja suddenly found herself in a position where she did not have to work. More importantly, she could care for Genowefa. She bought her mother new clothes and had new appliances delivered to their home. Genowefa welcomed their good fortune.

In her next letter Shoshana invited Alicja to visit her and her family in New York. How wonderful, Genowefa told Alicja, that she'd found relatives after all this time and could perhaps visit some of them in America. Genowefa couldn't help sharing the exciting news with some of her friends and neighbors.

"What a thing to happen to my Ala," she beamed.

"Yes," one of the women, the wife of a Bochnia police officer, agreed. "What a thing."

Forty-three

September 2004
WARSAW, POLAND

L ucia sat pensively in a Warsaw café with Mitchell, nervously tapping a spoon on her coffee cup. Over a year had passed since the conference in Washington, D.C. Lucia still couldn't get the question out of her head: *if everything was so perfect at home, why did you leave?*

"What's wrong?" Mitchell asked.

"I have something to tell you. . .it's not easy for me to talk about.

They were waiting for Olaf Zylicz, a Polish psychology professor from Warsaw they'd met at another conference in Washington, D.C., a few months earlier. Olaf was collaborating on a book about altruism, intergroup apology, forgiveness, and reconciliation. Lucia and Mitchell had formed a friendly bond with Olaf at the conference and arranged to visit him on their next trip to Poland.

"What is it?" Mitchell grew concerned. It was clearly a serious matter.

"What you know about my childhood is not everything that there is to know."

Mitchell knew a great deal about his mother's childhood.

"What else is there to know?" he asked.

"It's about Franciszek."

"Franciszek?"

With great difficulty, Lucia told Mitchell about Franciszek's advances when she reached adolescence, how she lived in almost daily fear of him, and how, after she rejected his advances, he had distanced himself from her, refusing to help her attend university, or even find a job. "He was committed to Krakow and his mistresses," Lucia whispered, "more than he was to me and my mother."

By the time she finished, Lucia was in tears. And Mitchell was stunned. Both Franciszek and Genowefa had been heroes to him. He'd always imagined his mother living in a safe home, with Franciszek providing a haven from the difficulties of her life in Bochnia. Now he learned that her childhood home was not the protective bubble he'd pictured. Apparently her challenges had not ended when she came home from school and walked past Chmielewski's door. He wondered how she had managed to keep herself together through it all. He rose from his chair and gave his mother a hug.

"Are you all right?" he asked before returning to his seat. She nodded quietly. Something in her seemed to relax.

"It's such a relief to get this off my chest," she said.

Just then Olaf entered the café.

Forty-four

Winter 1961
BOCHNIA, POLAND

When Alicja next met the man from Krakow who had been giving her envelopes from Shoshana Twersky, she broached the subject of visiting New York. His expression was not encouraging.

"You would need a tourist visa," he said. "I can try to help you get one, but it's almost impossible to get one to visit the United States. It's tough enough just to get a visa to Czechoslovakia or Hungary, but to get one to the United States. . .Communist officials would not only reject it, they'd interrogate you to find out who you are and why you want to go there. I could perhaps get you a tourist visa to Belgium. From there it may be possible to get to America."

Alicja mentioned her application for a tourist visa to Belgium when she next visited with Jewish agency representatives. They had been persistent in trying to convince her to go to Israel. They stiffened when she told them she was holding off on a decision until after she visited her relatives in New York.

"We are familiar with a certain individual who is dealing with American money and making visa promises," one said sternly. "Do not, under any circumstances, get involved with that man."

Alicja nodded obediently. She didn't want to jeopardize her relationship with the agency, but she was determined to go to New York.

When she next met with Shoshana's contact, she asked about the travel visa to Belgium. He told her he had applied for one, but the application had been rejected. "Perhaps it's a clerical error," he tried to soothe her. "No worries. I'll reapply immediately."

But this second application was also rejected, and this time the word "FINAL" was stamped in large red letters over the face of the document. No explanation was given.

So Genowefa accompanied Alicja on the long trip to the Polish Ministry of Travel in Warsaw to find out the reason. A clerk spoke with them, then went to a cabinet and ruffled through some files. He removed a dog-eared document, perused it for a while and put it back. His disappointed look when he returned told them the news was not good.

"This is off the record," he whispered. "Do you understand?" They nodded. "I'm also Jewish. I'm sorry to tell you that from what I see in your file, they'll never allow you to leave the country for any reason."

Alicja could not hide her bitter disappointment. "But why?"

"I can't be sure," the clerk said, "but it looks like your name was put on notice by the police in Bochnia. That's where the trouble started."

Genowefa's face reddened, realizing she'd been betrayed by her neighbor, the policeman's wife.

"Your only chance of leaving," the clerk continued, "is to change your official identity and register with the authorities as a Jew. You could then apply for a visa to Israel. But it would not be a tourist visa, you must understand. It would be an emigration visa. It would mean that you would have to give up your Polish citizenship." Alicja and Genowefa listened in stunned silence.

"And even if you do all that I have said," he cautioned, "I can't promise it will work."

On the three-hour return trip to Bochnia, Alicja reflected on her future. What kind of life would she have if she stayed in Poland? Yet the idea of emigrating was so final. She leaned her head against the train window, wishing she could be transported beyond the confinements of the train, beyond the predicament of her life. Emigrate? To Israel? Leaving Genowefa behind? She could not bear the thought.

Alicja put her hand in Genowefa's.

"We're not going to give up," Genowefa said.

Alicja nodded but took her worries to bed. One night around this time she dreamed that a cloud-like figure dragged her away from her bed and away from her home. She was shaken by the dream, but chose not to tell Genowefa about it. It was only a dream, she told herself the following morning.

Forty-five

September 2004
WARSAW/BOCHNIA/SZEBNIE, POLAND

Olaf Zylicz, the man meeting Lucia and Mitchell in War-saw, was raised a Christian, but was greatly influenced by a Jewish family friend. He said his identity "had never been made fully clear" to him. Years earlier he'd assembled a small community, a *havurah*, of Christians with similar identity questions. They began practicing some of the Jewish Shabbat rituals.

Before leaving for Bochnia, Olaf invited Lucia and Mitchell to his home for Shabbat, where he led his wife and young children through a stirring round of *zemirot*, *kiddush* and *ha'motzi*. He also invited a friend, a middle-age communications executive who had recently learned she was Jewish. It was one of the most moving Shabbat dinners they ever experienced.

After the Sabbath, Olaf accompanied Lucia and Mitchell to Bochnia. They visited the Swiateks' gravesites and Lucia's old church, St. Mikolaj. They also toured her gymnazjum, where a photo of her former mentor, Director Bernacki, was still proudly displayed. Then they went to Lucia's childhood home.

Mitchell surveyed the exterior of the house, gazing at the balcony where, as a little girl, Lucia had almost been struck by a brick thrown at her by her landlord. He spotted the alley adjacent to

Chmielewski's apartment through which Lucia had to pass to reach her own apartment. He had long fantasized about finding him and avenging the pain he caused his mother. He guessed Chmielweski was dead by now; nevertheless he wanted to knock on the front door of his old apartment.

"Perhaps his relatives still live here," he told Lucia, and headed towards the door.

"Mitchell, come back here!" Lucia called out.

He turned around, feeling like a little boy being scolded for venturing into forbidden territory.

"What are you going to do if someone answers?" Lucia asked.

"I don't know exactly. Ask if they are related to Chmielewski?"

"Why? What's the point?"

But Mitchell was insistent.

Lucia relented. "Perhaps Olaf could knock on the door if this is so important to you."

Olaf agreed. Lucia reached for Mitchell's hand and took several steps back towards the street as Olaf approached the door. After a gentle knock, an elderly woman appeared behind the partially opened door. From where they stood, Mitchell and Lucia could hear Olaf and the woman speaking but could not decipher what was being said. From the expression on the woman's face, it was clear that their presence was not welcome. In the next moment, the woman shook her head vigorously and slammed the door shut. Olaf retreated and met Lucia and Mitchell on the street.

"Let's get out of here," he said. "I felt the force of evil there."

Neither of them asked what the old woman had said to Olaf. As Olaf drove away from Lucia's childhood home, Lucia was glum. Mitchell wanted to linger in other parts of Bochnia, but Lucia wanted to leave as soon as possible. This was no nostalgic homecoming.

"We came here for Mitchell," Lucia told Olaf. "Now there's a place I need to go—for *me*. I want to go to Szebnie, where I believe my parents were taken."

After months of forced labor and mass executions, the final liquidation of the Bochnia ghetto began on September 1, 1943. There was a selection where the children and the elderly were immediately taken to Auschwitz. About one thousand able-bodied Jews between the ages of thirteen to thirty-five were then transferred by train the next day to a concentration camp in Szebnie for hard labor.

In October, about two hundred women were taken away from Szebnie in trucks and executed. Men, who had been brought with them in order to burn the bodies were then shot as well. The camp was liquidated just weeks later, on November 7th, when hundreds were herded out to a nearby forest and executed. Any Jews remaining were gathered at the train station, ordered to strip and transported to Auschwitz in open cattle cars.

It was about a two-hour drive to Szebnie from Bochnia. The narrow road was scenic; on either side lush green countryside dotted with farms and villages gleamed under the clear blue sky. It took some time to find the site of the Szebnie concentration camp. A school now stood in its place.

Lucia, Mitchell, and Olaf went into the main office, where a cheerful, heavyset woman introduced herself as Teresa Krol, the school principal. They explained the reason for their visit, and she responded graciously. She gave them a tour of her school, expressing pride in her students' accomplishments. Then she took them to a small room where she maintained a mini-museum of sorts—a collection of prison camp documents, weapons, and uniforms.

Teresa told them she had been a teenager during the war

and still recalled with great angst the horror of those times. She took them outside and pointed towards a roadway with a stream running alongside it. Beyond there were trees.

"Down there, we heard the gunshots every day," she said. "Constant gunshots. And later the horrible smell of burning bodies. Sometimes we'd see bones floating down the stream. It was so horrible. I can take you to the site. There's a plaque dedicated to the victims."

She led them beyond the stream and through the trees to a clearing.

"Look around," she said. "Around us everything is green. But here nothing grows. Not since then."

She led them to a small granite plaque memorializing those who died there. Olaf and Mitchell donned *kippot*, lit a *yahrzheit* candle, and began reciting the Kaddish prayer.

Lucia stood on the ground where her father had likely died in a hail of bullets. She gazed at the flame pulsating inside the *yahrzheit* candle. Deep emotion welled up inside, but no tears came. She felt again the painful sense of orphanhood that had marked her life. In her mind she spoke to her father; perhaps he was listening to her here in this forsaken place.

Why did you leave me behind? It might have been better had you taken me with you instead of leaving me to struggle on my own. She vacillated between determination and despair. *There is a reason,* she told herself, choosing determination. *There is a reason.*

Olaf and Mitchell finished reciting the Kaddish. Then each of them held Lucia's hand and they walked out of the forest and back onto the main street.

Forty-six

Spring 1961
BOCHNIA POLAND

A licja didn't know who to turn to for help with her visa problem. Then she thought about Director Bernacki, who was now retired from the school. He was her most ardent supporter, almost a father figure, in her years at the gymnazjum. She hadn't seen him since graduation. But it seemed natural to turn to him now for guidance and support, which he had always given her so generously.

After arranging an appointment by phone, Alicja arrived at Director Bernacki's home, a simple single-floor dwelling about a thirty minute walk from her home. Upon opening the door and seeing Alicja, he threw his arms around her with delight. He invited her inside and the directed her to the round kitchen table, where a plate of pastries, a bowl of fruit, and two cups for tea were set. Director Bernacki looked like he had aged more than just the few years that had passed; he appeared to be ailing from some disease.

"I was sad to hear that you were unable to continue on to university," he said.

"I have a much more serious problem now," Alicja responded.

She explained her predicament: she could drop her visa request and settle for a life in Poland, with no telling what kind of life that would be, or she could seek to immigrate to Israel. If the Jewish agency and the Lawaszes were to be believed, Israel held brighter opportunities for her future, but it was still a future without Genowefa.

Director Bernacki sympathized. "It doesn't appear that there is a middle ground here. Perhaps Israel is the only way," he sighed.

"But I don't want it to be permanent. I don't want to give up my Polish citizenship. I want to be able to come back and see Mama."

"Hmmm," Director Bernacki muttered. "Perhaps there is another way. Another former student of mine is now a government official. He might be able to help. I'll speak to him about your situation and see what he says."

Several days later Director Bernacki called Alicja. He told her his former student had agreed to meet with her and Genowefa in his office in Krakow. He said he would accompany Alicja and her mother there by train to meet with him.

The meeting in the government official's office was strained. The official seemed genuinely happy to see Director Bernacki, but not happy to see Alicja and her mother. Director Bernacki explained their situation, but the official showed no sympathy and offered no hint of intended helpfulness. When Director Bernacki was finished, the official asked to speak with Alicja alone. Genowefa and Director Bernacki left the office to wait outside. As soon as the door closed behind them he gave Alicja a stern look.

"Sit down," he hissed. "I'm going to do what I can, but only because of the high regard I have for Director Bernacki. And there is no guarantee I'll be able to do anything." He moved closer and towered over her. "But you should be ashamed of yourself for bringing such a sick man all the way to Krakow for your own selfish interests. And what's more, you should be ashamed for thinking about leaving a woman who saved your life, and who is obviously sick herself." Alicja looked down guiltily; he was only telling her things she had already told herself. "You disgust me," he concluded. "Now go."

Genowefa and Director Bernacki were pacing the hallway when Alicja emerged from the office.

"What's wrong?" Genowefa asked. "You're white as a ghost."

"Nothing, Mama," she replied. "He said he would help. I guess I'm just overwhelmed by all of this."

Forty-seven

Be aware of your steps as they are guided through your dreams
Believe in the power of your soul.

—Lucia's journal, May 1999

January 2005–April 2006
NEW YORK, NY

Lucia's revelation about Franciszek reminded Mitchell that his mother needed someone with objectivity and distance to help her peel away the layers of her protective shell and address traumatic events still buried there. Lucia agreed.

Lucia again contacted Catherine Shainberg. Shainberg responded this time, but was unavailable as a mentor. Instead, she referred Lucia to a warm, intuitive writer named Gay Walley. Shainberg and Walley had collaborated on a recent book, *Kabbalah and the Power of Dreaming.*

Lucia was reluctant to meet Walley. She had opened up to far too many people already. But Gay, the child of a Holocaust survivor mother who had abandoned her as an infant, quickly proved to be a sensitive and empathetic companion.

Meanwhile Lucia's journal entries were beginning to resemble a working manuscript. She needed literary as well as spiritual guidance. The timing with Gay could not have been better. The two spent countless draining hours talking and reflecting. Gay wasn't just interviewing Lucia—she was absorbing her experiences.

"Lucia, I can't imagine how difficult this must be for you," Gay said repeatedly during those first meetings. "This isn't just a book about dreams and visions. You're not trying to analyze dreams. You're having a dialogue with God. And though I am no theologian, from what I know about the Bible, those who have had a dialogue with God do not have an easy road."

"Yes," Lucia responded, although she'd never thought of her experience in those terms before. "I guess that's true."

Feeling increasingly liberated to open more deeply and share her experiences, Lucia began to dream and write again with even greater intensity. She recorded one of two dreams she had early in her work with Gay.

> *I am wearing a white cotton dress, getting soaked in a pouring rain, even though the skies are clear. In an instant, my white dress is replaced by a gold one.*

The rain, Lucia knew, symbolized cleansing and transformation. Clearly she'd been going through a transformation over the last several years. But the gold dress in her dream was curious. Gold was a repeating motif in her dreams and visions. She'd had a vision with golden light, and she'd dreamed of a golden envelope, but it was still not clear what this dream meant.

And then she had a second dream in which a woman appeared wearing an elaborate gold dress, a contrast to the simple one she was wearing in the earlier dream.

Once again, seeking answers to the questions arising out of these dreams, she turned to her journal. Opening its pages, she was inspired to write:

> *When you find the gold dress and the woman behind the dress, your life will change forever.*

Lucia sighed. She didn't question the authenticity of what she'd written, but she didn't understand it either. She would have to be patient. Mystical mysteries, she knew by now, were revealed in their own time.

In the first months of 2006, Lucia felt as if her life was changing, and that her search for the woman behind the dress was indeed a search for a solution to everything she'd struggled with for so long—an identity that was true to who she was, and an understanding of the meaning and purpose of her life.

A series of three dreams Lucia had from February though April 2006 amplified her sense that a new, powerful phase of her journey was unfolding. Lucia's first dream entry reads:

> *I am at a performance. A cantor is singing on stage. He suddenly stops singing—he's forgotten what he's about to sing. A moment later, he collapses and dies. I visit his gravesite and place a single pink rose on the grave.*

The dream was mystifying to her. Who was the cantor? What was the significance of his sudden collapse and death? And what did the rose represent?

The questions remained unanswered. Then she had the second dream:

> *I am in a bank and enter the back room where there is a large vault. I try several keys but I cannot open the vault. I then empty a big shopping bag on a table. A bunch of red beets—still attached to their stems—pour out. I start cleaning up the mess and find a gold key hidden among the stems. I take the key back to the vault and insert the key. This time, the vault opens. There is no jewelry or other valuables inside. Instead, I find a stack of papers and a Social Security card. I close the vault and leave the bank. I become aware of a warning that the vault in this bank is not safe and that its contents need to be removed. Herman appears outside and directs me to a site across the street where a new building is being constructed.*

Once again, the dream was mystifying. Lucia had recently had her purse stolen with all her credit cards in it. Was the dream, replete with the theme of security, simply a reflection of her recent experience? She considered the possibility but dismissed it as too simplistic. What about the red beets? Or the stack of papers and the social security card? And it just wasn't *any* key that opened the vault. It was a *gold* key. Surely, she thought, there was a deeper meaning to the dream than stolen credit cards.

A short time later, she had a third dream:

All four of us—me, Mitchell, Lisa, and Herman—are enjoying ourselves at some sort of happy occasion. We are having fun. I sense that Herman dies. I tell him that I'm so happy that he had fun with us, if only for a little while. But Mitchell is upset and leaves the room. When he returns, I tell him that we need to go to another room to see Herman being prepared for burial. We arrive at the room and see a body lying on a table, covered in a white veil. I approach the table and remove the veil. But it is not Herman's body underneath the veil; it is the body of a young woman, very much alive, and smiling.

This third dream provoked still more questions, but Lucia now began to find a thread, a theme that connected the dreams to each other, and to her journey.

She surmised that the cantor's abrupt passing in her first dream represented something that was unknown or unrevealed—in essence, something locked in a vault of the sort that appeared in her second dream. What exactly was unknown or unrevealed remained a mystery. But if the social security card in the second dream represented her identity, an identity that was changing and evolving, she was certain that what was not yet revealed would be so in the future.

She considered that the young woman's unveiling in her third dream represented a shift in her identity and spiritual consciousness. It was *she* who was being unveiled!

Lucia felt exhilarated at solving the mysteries of her dream, yet she was still apprehensive. Security, or a lack thereof, loomed large in all three dreams—in the cantor's sudden collapse; in the supposedly safe bank vault deemed unsafe by her husband, Herman; and in an initially happy family scene disrupted by the specter of death and burial.

What did all of this mean for her? She rarely felt secure at any point in her life, not as a frightened child in Bochnia, and not as a wife who fretted over Herman's frequent ill health. After Herman's death, a path to security presented itself on several occasions. Friends had been eager to match her with suitors. She'd been invited to numerous social gatherings. Yet she largely turned her back on it all, committed to a path of insecurity of *her* choice. Her pursuit of mystical decoding, of interpreting what she believed to be Divine communications, could hardly be more insecurity-inducing.

She pondered the other-worldliness of her dreams and her writing, and of her entire journey; and she pondered the significance of what she found in the bank vault of her second dream —the gold key.

Forty-eight

June 1961
BOCHNIA, POLAND

Alicja received a notice from the travel ministry indicating that a visa and passport would be available for pick-up at the Israeli embassy in Warsaw in several days. It was not the travel visa she'd hoped for, but an emigration visa. Genowefa, reading the notice, held back her tears.

When Franciszek learned that Alicja would be emigrating, a profound sense of remorse overtook him. He had been estranged from her for years, but when he asked her to accompany him on a walk early one morning, she tepidly agreed.

He led her out of the neighborhood on an unfamiliar route to a place she did not recognize. They reached a gate that opened to a desolate field overgrown with weeds and bushes. Why he had brought her here? She felt anxious.

Franciszek pointed to a small, barely noticeable inscription in the marble at the side of the gate, covered with spider webs. He brushed aside the webs to reveal a Star of David carved into the stone.

"This is the Jewish cemetery," he said. "Perhaps many generations of your family were buried here before the war."

Alicja surveyed the neglected, forsaken lot, a stark contrast to the lovingly, respectfully maintained Christian cemetery on the hill where she spent many hours of her childhood.

Franciszek turned to Alicja with a pained look.

"I brought you here to open my heart to you and to relieve your fears about the future. I am truly sorry, Alicja, for my abominable behavior, both to you and your mother."

Alicja searched for the appropriate emotional response. She knew she should be feeling anger and rage; she should curse him. No simple apology could make up for all the years of fear and suffering he had caused her and her mother. Yet she heard herself say, tentatively, "That's alright."

But Franciszek had not completed his apology. "I know I should have taken both of you out of that ditch a long, long time ago. I should have moved all of us out of Bochnia to a nice apartment in Krakow. You wouldn't have suffered so much."

She glanced up at Franciszek and saw his eyes welling with tears. She'd never seen that before. He spoke in a mournful voice.

"You're going to Israel. I've heard it's a beautiful, free country. Free of communism. You can speak out there. You can pursue dreams. If I could, I would go there with you."

He stood there before her, silent and ashamed. She recalled those moments when he had been her hero: when he'd taken the landlord to court to stop his abusive behavior towards her, and when he soothed her angst after the Easter Passion service at school.

This was the Franciszek she wished he'd been all along, the Franciszek who stayed hidden in Krakow. Had he not been so distant, had she not been so frightened to be alone with him, had he been more helpful in supporting her university ambitions or helped her find a good job, Genowefa would never have shaken that dresser and found that letter from her Jewish relative. And she would not be in the predicament she was in now. The terrible thought of leaving Genowefa brought her to tears, and a wave of anger rippled through her. But she did not want to be angry at her father. She wanted to love him.

"Papa," she whispered, surprised at finding her voice. 'I wish you could come with me to Israel."

Franciszek reached for Alicja's hand as they walked out of the Jewish cemetery. A little girl once again, she gave it to him.

Forty-nine

When you find the gold dress and the woman behind the dress, your life will change forever.

– Lucia's journal, January 2005

August 2007
NEW YORK, NY

More than ever, Lucia was looking back, connecting threads from her past, at the same time that her inspired writings and dreams were propelling her forward.

About ten years had passed since David Bass, Lisa's former boyfriend, had asked Lucia over lunch the question that had thrown her into upheaval.

"What did you do about Jesus?"

David had kept in touch with Lisa and Lucia over the years and made plans to see them on his forthcoming trip to New York. He was coming to commemorate the return of Gustav Klimt's 1907 masterpiece, *Portrait of Adele Bloch-Bauer I*, to the heir of its original pre-war Jewish owner.

The painting was confiscated by Nazi operatives in 1938, with some apprehension. Austrians regarded the painting as their Mona Lisa. But the Nazis considered the painting too modernist, the painter was a known friend of the Jews, and the painting's subject, socialite Adele Bloch-Bauer, was Jewish. Its cultural significance could not be erased. So, to resolve the Jewish dilemma, the Nazis tried to erase Adele's identity by changing the name of the painting to "Dame in Gold."

More than five decades later, David's friend Randy Schoenberg, grandson of a Viennese composer who fled the Nazis, won a lengthy and epic legal battle with the Austrian government that returned the painting to its rightful heir, Adele's niece, Maria (Bloch-Bauer) Altmann. In June 2006, philanthropist Ronald Lauder purchased the painting and put it on display in New York City's Neue Galerie.

Today, the painting's origins and its recovery have been publicized by Anne-Marie O'Connor's book, The *Lady in Gold: The Extraordinary Tale of Gustav Klimt's Masterpiece, Portrait of Adele Bloch-Bauer* and the film *Woman in Gold.* But in August 2007, Lucia was unfamiliar with the painting and its artist.

David met Lisa and Lucia at a café on the East Side. He greeted them warmly. After catching up with Lisa, he turned to Lucia.

"Take a look at this." He handed her a brochure from the Neue Galerie, where the painting would be on permanent display.

As Lucia looked in astonishment at the image of the painting, the words from her journal came back to her:

When you find the gold dress and the woman behind the dress, your life will change forever.

Was this the gold dress she'd seen in her second dream, the one with the image of a woman wearing a gold dress? What did the "woman *behind* the dress" mean? She couldn't be sure, but it was clear from this first viewing that the woman *in* the dress, the subject of the painting, was named Adele, her mother's name. She contemplated what this discovery meant for her. Surely the name Adele alone was not coincidental.

The next morning, she raced to the Neue Galerie and absorbed the painting. Its overwhelming gold tones evoked the sense of light that she'd experienced in her dreams of a gold envelope, a gold key, and a gold dress. The painting's Egyptian "all-seeing-eye" motif suggested a great mystical depth beyond the visibly material content of the subject; something elevated the painting into the spiritual realm.

She bought two books on the painting and the painter and devoured them. Klimt was a painter with a colorful history, varied spiritual interests and an intense fondness for women. Adele Bloch-Bauer was an ambitious woman who sought to defy the conventions of her time, a strong figure who transcended the material trappings depicted in the painting.

Adele Bloch-Bauer, a society woman born into privilege in Vienna in 1881, and Klimt, a Viennese-born painter whose unconventional and occasionally erotic works delighted (and sometimes outraged) his early-twentieth-century audiences, could not have come from more dissimilar backgrounds than Lucia, born in Bochnia, Poland, in the Nazi era. Yet Lucia now felt inexorably linked to them.

Fifty

June 1961
BOCHNIA, POLAND

Leaving the Jewish cemetery, Franciszek went to work. When Alicja told Genowefa about their conversation, her mother was heartened by the reconciliation, yet sad that it had come so late, with Alicja soon to leave, perhaps forever.

That afternoon Alicja left home and headed for the market. Two blocks away, as she was about to turn onto Rzeznocka Street, two uniformed men came up from behind her, one on each side of her.

"We need you to come with us to the police station," one of them said.

"What for?" Alicja asked, startled.

"We have a few questions about your visa."

They escorted her several blocks away and took her to a small, damp room with a table and several straight-backed chairs where two other uniformed men already sat waiting.

"Do you have the visa to Israel?" one tight-lipped official asked tersely.

"No, I don't."

"When do you expect to get it?"

"I don't know."

"Do you know a man named Blumstein?"

"No."

The official's face reddened. He leaned over menacingly, glaring at her.

"You are a liar. Were you not trying to obtain a visa to Belgium through him? To run to the United States? Did you not ask him to help smuggle you into the United States?"

"I. . ."

"Did you not contact the criminal Blumstein to help you plot your defection?" barked the second man, silent until now.

"No, I never wanted to desert my homeland," she found the strength to respond. "I only wanted to visit my relatives in New York."

"Do you know where your friend Blumstein is now?"

"No."

"He is in custody. Awaiting just punishment," said the first man. Alicja groaned. "Why did you lie to us a few minutes ago, saying you didn't know Blumstein?" demanded the second.

"I didn't lie," she cried out. "I never knew his name."

The men grew increasingly hostile. They seemed uninterested in her answers, impatiently peppering her with endless questions. They dragged the interrogation on for hours, well into the evening.

Earlier that afternoon another uniformed official had knocked at the Swiateks' door. Genowefa, who had grown increasingly worried when Alicja didn't return from the market, felt a moment of panic when she saw a police official standing there.

"I'm here to see Alicja Swiatek's visa to Israel. Please show it to me," he demanded.

"We don't have it; they never sent it," Genowefa told him. "Where is Alicja?"

"She's in custody," the official said severely.

Then he pushed past Genowefa into the house and began a

frenzied search, rifling through drawers, emptying closets and cabinets, looking under mattresses and pillows. When he left after finding no visa, Genowefa rushed out to see Director Bernacki. All the way there she was crying to herself, "They have Alicja! They have Alicja!"

Fifty-one

October 2007 - February 2008
NEW YORK, NY

L ucia closed the flap of another journal crammed with writings and notes. She wondered whether the dreams and visions would soon come to an end. It seemed that they might. In one dream, she found a gold key to unlock a vault, suggesting that the meaning of her experiences would shortly be revealed. In another, she removed a veil that covered the body of a young woman, presumably representing her. Surely this meant that she was ready to be transformed in some way. Perhaps that transformation was to begin now. The thought offered some relief. But a dream she had in October 2007 suggested otherwise:

> *I am in a blue compartment on a train going to Bochnia. I sense that a presence is with me and I ask if I am on the right road home. The presence answers that Bochnia is one kilometer up ahead. But the train is moving very slowly, and it stops just before the Bochnia station. It does not reach its destination.*

Lucia understood the train to be not just a means of transportation, but also a vehicle of communication, much like the golden envelope. She had read about the Jewish mystical tradition of the *merkaba* in Rodger Kamenetz's *The History of Last Night's Dream*. The word *merkaba* translates as "a thing to ride in" or "chariot." The merkaba tradition relates to Ezekiel's vision of the chariot of God driven by four winged beings. To Lucia, the train in her dream *was* a merkaba. And she had further to travel on it.

Several months later Lucia was watching a television program on the history of Jerusalem, broadcast in anticipation of the sixtieth anniversary of the establishment of the modern state of Israel. As the camera panned the Old City, inevitably zooming in on the golden Dome of the Rock and the Western Wall below, Lucia was compelled to reflect on her 1994 trip to the Wall, the first time she'd felt a sense of Divine communication. At the time, she thought she'd received a message telling her that a companion would appear in her life to alleviate her loneliness. She now knew that a much deeper communication had occurred.

When the television program ended, Lucia was inspired to write:

> *I will take you to the land of origin and marry you at the same site you made a covenant with me. You have followed my voice through your writing, the fruits of which you are to bring with you. The final words will come at the site. The book you are writing is your covenant with me. The golden light on its pages is confirmation that I am leading your pen and guiding you where you need to be. Open your heart to the one I am sending and follow my voice and record my words that have not been written yet. The voice you are hearing is the same as Abraham heard when he was following the road paved by me. You are not alone and were not meant to be. You needed to learn to hear my voice and recognize I am that I am.*

This passage contained many of the themes in her visions and dreams since that visit to the Wall fourteen years earlier. It confirmed her sense that her writing was Divinely inspired, that God was leading her pen. But it also overwhelmed her. And the idea making her story public only magnified her angst. She discussed her feelings with Mitchell on his next visit. So many images had come—a golden light, a golden envelope, a lion in the sky, an angel and Jesus in a circle of golden light, a golden key, a gold dress, many more, and now an unnerving reference to Abraham and "I am that I am"? Who was *she* to receive such communications?

"I didn't ask for this," she lamented.

"I know," Mitchell said.

"No one will believe this. They'll dismiss me. Call me crazy. Or worse."

"There will be people who will believe this and people who won't," he said. "But this is *your* truth. And no one can take that away from you."

Fifty-two

June 1961
BOCHNIA, POLAND

Director Bernacki rushed out of his home with Genowefa on their way to the police station. Genowefa entered the station first and darted to the front desk. The officer sitting behind the desk looked up from his newspaper.

"Where is Alicja? Where is my daughter?" Genowefa asked frantically.

"Wait here," he said. He got up and went through a door. A moment later two officials emerged. They ignored Genowefa and addressed Director Bernacki.

"The woman can wait here," one of them growled. "Director Bernacki, you may come with us."

They led him through the door, which closed behind them, leaving Genowefa alone. She paced frantically in the waiting area, wondering what was happening. The officer came out and returned to reading his newspaper behind the desk. Genowefa sat down to wait on a wooden bench against a wall. She glanced frequently at her watch. An hour passed slowly. Finally, one of the officials emerged from the door. Director Bernacki appeared behind her with Alicja, who looked shaken and pale.

"She is being released only until Monday, when she will

testify in the trial of Isaac Blumstein," the official said. Genowefa and Alicja gazed at each other fretfully.

"Ordinarily she would not have been released at all," he continued. "She is being released only under Director Bernacki's personal guardianship." This last statement was spoken emphatically, and with that he turned and disappeared through the door.

Director Bernacki walked Genowefa and Alicja back to their home. When they were out of sight of the police station he broke the tense silence.

"Don't say anything; just listen," he whispered. "They didn't tell me in so many words, but after you testify at the trial they plan on holding you indefinitely. I don't think they're going to allow you to go to Israel or anywhere else."

Alicja gasped. What had all of this come to? Was she to be a prisoner now? Forever? She wished she had never met the Twerskys' contact. She wished she could turn back the clock. They walked the last few blocks home in silence. When they entered the house Director Bernacki turned to her.

"Go pack a suitcase, Alicja," he ordered. "Quickly!"

"B-but. . ."

"Now, Alicja! Start packing now!" His voice was almost harsh, like a headmaster berating a disobedient student. "I'm sorry, Alicja." His tone softened. "I can't imagine how difficult this must be. But you must trust me and do what I tell you. I only want the best of everything for you, my dear, the best of everything."

"How can I thank you, Director Bernacki?

"Just keep making me proud, Alicja. As you always have. Now we must move quickly."

Franciszek arrived from Krakow as soon as he could, with

three train tickets in his hand. Director Bernacki had called to inform him about the troublesome turn of events. Alicja, Genowefa, and Franciszek took the last train out of Bochnia to Warsaw. They spent a sleepless Friday night in a hotel by Warsaw's central station.

The Israeli embassy was closed on Saturday, the Jewish Sabbath. Franciszek, Genowefa, and Alicja paced the city streets together, painfully aware of the danger of Alicja's capture, and of their imminent separation. Sunday morning brought a relative respite from the tension: the Israeli embassy was open at the same time that the Polish government offices were closed. They went to the Israeli embassy and picked up Alicja's visa and passport, which were waiting for her behind the counter. Franciszek put Alicja's documents in his pants pocket. As they walked out onto the street he stayed several yards behind Alicja, just in case they were under surveillance and she was approached.

At sundown they boarded a train bound for Vienna through Czechoslovakia. Without visas to enter, Genowefa and Franciszek would have to disembark at the border.

Alicja rested her head on Genowefa's shoulders and closed her eyes, exhausted yet unable to sleep. Genowefa stroked her hair, and occasionally glanced in despair at Franciszek.

Hours later the train slowed down and emerged from the darkness into a lantern-lit station. A Czechoslovakian official announced that they had arrived at the border, and asked passengers to show their travel papers. Franciszek handed Alicja her Israeli visa and passport. The official came by, inspected her documents, handed them back and moved on.

The moment they had all dreaded arrived. They embraced each other with the force of a lifetime shared together. Genowefa and Franciszek stepped off the train onto the station platform. The train whistle blew and the doors closed. Alicja leaned against the window facing the platform. A lantern cast shadows of the two solitary figures waving their hands. The train began to rumble along the track and Franciszek and Genowefa soon faded from her sight. Then she was alone.

Two Bochnia policemen came to the Swiateks' home first thing Monday morning.

"Where is your daughter?" one officer demanded.

"How should I know?" Franciszek replied. "She's twenty-one-years old. A twenty-one year-old girl is bound to be anywhere."

Fifty-three

April 2008
NEW YORK, NY

Three days before Passover, Lucia again dreamed and recorded in her journal a sequence of three apparently related dreams. The first dream reads,

> *I see a golden eagle descending from the sky. It embraces me with its wings, and then gently presses its beak against my face. A group of people watch this in awe. I cherish the moment, holding onto it as long as the moment will allow.*

The second dream reads,

> *I am peeling two hard-boiled brown eggs. I break apart the eggs and eat the yolks.*

The third dream reads,

> *I am on a train to Bochnia. This time the train stops there and I walk to my home. I look for Genowefa but cannot find her. But I do see Franciszek. He is lying down in bed, ill. There is someone else in the home—a large black woman. I embrace her with love.*

Several weeks after the dreams, Lucia spoke to Mitchell about them.

"You can already guess what the golden eagle represented," she said, teacher to student.

"A messenger," Mitchell said. "Just as the golden envelope was."

"Yes," Lucia nodded. "The golden eagle is the bird that flies closest to the sun. It's a messenger of Divine light."

Mitchell leaned forward in his chair. "And what was the message?"

"Actually, there are several messages. One message is liberation."

"Liberation? Ahh—Passover. The dream took place around Passover, a holiday of liberation."

"That's a start. I feel like I've been liberated—from the fear that consumed me while I was in Poland, the fear of losing your father, and the fear of exploring and expressing who I really am. Now, what about the eggs in my dream?"

"I know that eggs are a symbol of Passover," said Mitchell. "Some say they represent Temple sacrifice; others say they point to rebirth, the circular nature of life, and the infiniteness of God, who is without beginning or end."

"Yes." Lucia nodded. "But there's more to it than that. I did not eat the *entire* egg in my dream; I ate *only* the yolks—two golden yolks. If there is ego and spirit, humanity and Divinity, then the golden yolks represent the Divine nature, or Divine sustenance. And when I ate and digested them, they became one in my body. The divisions that I've felt for so long disappeared. I felt whole. I was one. And this led to the last dream of going home to Bochnia. Now that I was whole, I could go home. I could not do so earlier. I was not ready."

Mitchell pondered Lucia's explanation. He had watched her struggle with deep inner conflicts and divisions over the years. Were these now resolved? Had her wounds been healed?

"So what was message of the dreams?" he asked.

"Love." Lucia uttered the single word with stunning simplicity. "The golden eagle embraced me with Divine love. I cannot help but feel love."

"How can there be love?" Mitchell asked. "After all you've been through?"

"It's not that there is no recollection of hurt or pain in my life," Lucia said gently. "Franciszek was in my dream for a reason. But the large black woman in the dream was a symbol of mother-love, the most powerful force in the universe."

Mitchell gazed at his mother. How nearly unrecognizable she'd become since his father had died. The golden eagle dream and its message of love seemed to him a kind of culmination of her journey.

But every completion was also a new beginning.

"I now believe that as much as it *is* personal, this is not *just* a personal journey," she said. "I am being given messages to share with others. I don't know what it all means yet. I may never know. But there's still much work to be done."

She reached into her purse and removed a photocopy of a passage she found that was inspired by the *Song of Solomon*. She handed it to Mitchell to read:

The Divine Sun has shone upon me
Hath looked upon me
My light has become so dazzling
That in your unilluminated state
You cannot interpret what you see
And I appear to you to be black

Fifty-four

June 1961
PETACH TIKVA, ISRAEL

After arriving by train to Vienna, Austria, Alicja boarded the *SS Hercules* and set sail for Israel. The Jewish agency in Krakow had once used the term *aliyah*, and she now heard it again as the ship approached the Israeli shoreline. Aliyah literally means to go up, to rise, suggesting that for a Jew, the act of moving to Israel is an elevation of spirit.

Alicja, though, was in descent, her head bowed as she pondered her uncertain future. She already missed Genowefa and Franciscek and her home.

She was met at the Port of Haifa by Sarah Barterer, her great-aunt, and Sarah's husband, Herschel. They recalled how their own daughter, at about Alicja's age, had made aliyah, joining Israel's pioneers and settling into a kibbutz. With zeal and picks, hoes and shovels, they tilled the land and freed themselves from a heritage of European pogroms. Sarah and her husband followed their daughter to Israel soon after. By now few traces of their Polish roots remained.

From Haifa, the Barterers shuttled Alicja towards their home in the Tel Aviv suburb of Petach Tikvah, which meant "gateway of hope." As Alicja gazed out the car window, she was surprised at the green landscape. Olive and willow trees lined the hilly terrain, sloping into peaceful meadows. Israel was, so far, not what she had long imagined: a cast of orphans shackled inside dark, windowless buildings.

The urban clustering of Tel Aviv soon overwhelmed the countryside. Alicja hoped to tour her new surroundings, but the Barterers explained that it would not be possible immediately. She arrived on a Friday, and as observant Jews, they had to prepare for the Sabbath.

At sundown, the hectic pace of the workweek and the rush to clean, cook, and dress for Shabbat came to a deliberate halt. Alicja tried to absorb the rituals: Sarah lit two large white candles, made three circular motions with the palms of her hand, as if drawing the light from the flames into her body, and recited a blessing. Her husband chanted a prayer over a goblet of wine. Over dinner, they explained some of the basic rules of Shabbat: no use of electricity, no turning on lights, the stove, or the television. No driving a car or riding a bus, either. No weekday-type work was to be performed and no money could be earned or spent. It would take some time, they explained, for her to learn the various rules and customs.

Alicja wondered how she would cope with an entire day of the Shabbat rules in her new home. To her surprise, she did more than cope. She found the stillness of Shabbat peaceful, even liberating. Like Bochnia on a Sunday morning, houses of worship in the little enclave of Petach Tikva were flush with people while buses stood idle and shops remained closed.

At sunset, the Barterers lit a braided candle and said a prayer over spices and wine. The Havdalah service marked the end of the Sabbath, a separation of the holiness of the Sabbath day and the ordinariness of the weekday. Alicja found herself reluctantly saying good-bye to Shabbat, not quite ready to let go of its soothing spirit.

Two weeks after she arrived in Israel, the Barterers enrolled Alicja in a nearby ulpan, a school for intensive Hebrew study. There she befriended a young Jewish couple from Hungary who had recently made aliyah and a group of South African Christians who had arrived in Israel several weeks earlier.

With her new friends she surveyed the Israeli landscape and marveled at its diversity. Jews, Christians, Arabs, Druze, and Armenians walked her streets speaking a myriad of languages. Alicja relished the taste of new foods like falafel and baklava.

Alicja was most surprised, though, by the diversity within the Jewish community, especially the divide between those who were religious and the majority of Israelis who were secular. She'd imagined only pious, bearded men and modestly clad women living in the Holy Land. But the beaches and clubs along Tel Aviv's shoreline presented a very different image.

She also learned that the Israeli workweek was six days, and that Friday night was the one occasion when most Israelis felt they could let loose, stay out late, and sleep in on Saturday before another workweek began on Sunday. Most Israelis did not observe the kind of Shabbat that she'd experienced with the Barterers.

Her South African Christian friends, though, were not bound by Friday night Jewish religious restrictions. They began exploring the Tel Aviv nightlife scene and invited Alicja to join them. It was a tempting offer. She'd been living with the elder Barterers for some time and was eager to enjoy recreation with her peers. She asked for some time to think about it.

On a slow walk back to the Barterers' home from the ulpan, Alicja pondered her choice. In Bochnia, she never considered not observing a church holiday in favor of a recreation pursuit. And on Sunday, the Sabbath day, she always went to services. If, as she was slowly acclimating to Jewish life, the Sabbath now meant Friday night into Saturday instead of Sunday, if it meant synagogue instead of a church, it was still the Sabbath. And the Sabbath was God's day.

Going out on the town was no way to acknowledge God's day, she decided. So she declined her friends' invitation. As she did, she thought about one other practical reason for doing so. Her goal was still to be with the Twerskys, her Orthodox relatives, in New York. The last thing in the world they should ever find out about would be her spending a Shabbat evening in a nightclub. Alicja was not about to compromise her future for that.

In December, the entire Barterer family gathered for Chanukah. Growing up, Alicja had never heard of the holiday commemorating the rededication of the Jerusalem Temple in 165 B.C.E., a victory over the Syrian-Greeks. The gathering was a joyous one; an array of colorful candles was placed on menorot, and trays of potato latkes, pancakes, and *sufganiot*—jelly donuts—were prepared. After the candles were lit, the youngest Barterer, a three-year-old girl, proudly sang the traditional "Ma'oz Tsur."

"Isn't she precious?" Alicja heard one of the grandmothers say.

Alicja took a bite of a potato latke—the first thing she'd eaten since the celebration began. An adolescent girl, a cousin she had not yet met, gazed inquisitively at her.

"Hey, aren't you the one who went to church?" the girl asked with satisfaction, as if she just solved a great mystery. "My mother told me about you. But I don't understand how you ever could have prayed to Jesus."

Alicja didn't respond. She moved away from the girl, leaving the rest of her plate of latkes untouched. And she found herself yearning for Christmas to arrive.

The scent of Christmas, so pervasive in Poland in late December, was nearly absent outside the Christian enclaves within Israel. Alicja longed for the scent of pine, for the familiar Christmas carols, and for Genowefa and Franciszek.

So when her friends from South Africa invited her to join them on Christmas Eve she gratefully accepted. She told the Barterers she was going to see her Hungarian Jewish friends that evening. The familiar carols soothed her angst, and the Chanukah songs and questions about praying to Jesus slowly drifted into the December night air.

Returning to the Barterers' home, Alicja slipped under the covers. Lying in the dark she remembered something that Franciszek often said: "God is everywhere." Maybe, Alicja thought, but I'm not sure where to find Him just now.

But Alicja set her spiritual angst aside when she learned that Shoshana Twersky and her husband would be visiting Israel in two weeks. This was the opportunity she'd been waiting for. Perhaps they would take her back with them to New York! She had no great desire to remain in Israel. More than that, she'd grown to feel intensely connected to the woman she called Aunt Shoshana. She liked Sarah Barterer, but it was Shoshana who'd put flesh on the bones of her family, linking her to a heritage that was one perhaps she could even be proud of.

Shoshana and her family embodied prominence and success, and Alicja had yearned for her place in the photographs of elegant homes and stylish portraits they sent her. Shoshana's life in New York was everything that the life of a girl sleeping on a straw bed in Bochnia was not.

Shoshana arrived at the Barterer's home on a Tuesday afternoon. Upon meeting each other, Alicja and Shoshana embraced like mother and daughter. Shoshana wore a powder blue sequined dress and a pale white shawl. She was as elegant as Alicja had imagined. Standing next to Shoshana, keeping a warm but religiously ordained distance from Alicja, was her husband, Abraham, who Alicja simply called "Uncle." His long, almost completely grey beard had curious streaks of stubborn black hair, perhaps a testament to his own strength and survival instincts; he saved his family from the German invasion some twenty years earlier.

The Barterers had only glowing things to say to the Twerskys about Alicja. They said she was a wonderful girl who conducted herself with dignity and grace, and they were pleased to have her in their home. Aunt Shoshana and Uncle beamed with pride. Alicja could practically see the New York harbor. But there was concern. Shoshana's niece, who had moved to Israel several years earlier and was secular, wondered how Alicja would cope in her aunt's ultra-Orthodox community.

"Alicja is a wonderful girl," she told Shoshana. "But she's so raw, so unexposed to what you are bringing her to in New York. I fear that she'll be overwhelmed."

Shoshana nodded, pondering her niece's comment.

"Perhaps it would be best to have her remain in Israel, at least for awhile longer," the niece continued. "Here she can adjust to life as a Jew at her own pace. She can attend university. She can shape her life as she wants to."

"But I have an obligation to her," Shoshanna countered. "I began this process in Poland and I need to see it through. Is there a greater mitzvah than to bring a girl like Alicja to yiddishkeit?"

"It is a tremendous mitzvah," her niece acknowledged. "But would you really be doing what's best for her?"

Others in their family had expressed similar concerns. Shoshana allowed her thoughts to settle for a few days. She picked a moment when she, Sarah Barterer, and her niece were preparing a meal in the Barterers' kitchen to bring up the subject, hoping it would be muffled by the clanging pots and simmering stew.

But Alicja heard from the living room what Shoshana was suggesting quite clearly—that perhaps it was best to leave Alicja in Israel for a while instead of bringing her to New York. Alicja's throat tightened and she strained to draw in a breath. This couldn't be. Not Shoshana. Not her last hope. She wanted to cry, to scream, to lay bawling on the floor like a toddler. She wanted to call Genowefa. But she couldn't do any of that. She had never allowed herself to be ungrateful for anything Genowefa or Franciszek had done for her. And she couldn't allow herself to be ungrateful now for all that Aunt Shoshana had done. But she could not be silent, either. So she went into the kitchen.

"I want to be with you, Aunt Shoshana," her voice sputtered. "I want to be with your family in New York."

Shoshana's head drooped. "Perhaps it would be best if you stayed in Israel for just a little while longer," she said without conviction, as though her heart was telling her otherwise.

Alicja took a decisive step toward the two elder women, one that bore the weight of her future.

"I won't stay in Israel," she declared. "I'll return to Poland."

Shoshana relented. She promised that when she returned to New York she would arrange to get Alicja a student visa to come to New York and study in the Bais Yaakov, a religious school for women.

Alicja joyfully began making preparations to go to New York, but asked Shoshana if she could take a slight detour on her way there. She had learned that she had another relative in Brussels, Belgium. And a family living in Antwerp had been close to her mother, Adele. She would like meet them, she told Shoshana, because she wasn't sure if she'd ever get another chance to do so. Shoshana agreed.

As Alicja waved good-bye to the Barterers and boarded an airplane bound for Belgium, she envisioned a map of Europe. Brussels lay about two thousand miles to the west of Tel Aviv, and Antwerp about thirty-two miles north of Brussels. About five hundred miles to the east is Bochnia, Poland—close enough, perhaps, to visit Genowefa and Franciszek.

Fifty-five

August 2008
NEW YORK, NY

You have followed my voice through your writing, the fruits of which you are to bring with you.

— From Lucia's journal, February 2008

Lucia had not forgotten her inspired writing from February 2008, in which she had been directed by the same voice that Abraham heard to "bring the fruits of her writing" (she assumed this referred to her manuscript) to the Western Wall in Jerusalem. She made no plans to travel there; trepidation, not procrastination, held her back. Who was *she* to hear God's voice?

But a dream she had in August during the somber holiday of Tisha B'Av, a fast day observed to commemorate the destruction of both Jerusalem temples, told her it was time to follow the direction she was given, her reservations notwithstanding. She recorded her dream:

I am at the Second Jerusalem Temple. I walk up many steps and approach a tall, double bronze door. There are tall columns on both sides of the door. An old man with grey hair and a white beard, wearing a white shirt, opens the door and lets me in. I am aware of myself going through the door. I see a beautiful landscape and a stream. I follow a path along the stream and approach a small bridge. I see the silhouette of someone I think is Jesus above the bridge. I go back and rest under a tree. Someone presents me with a gift—a shield with the Star of David on it. I walk back though the doorway and again find myself between the same two marble columns. I see Jesus walking beside someone who is wearing a red cloak and is barefoot. I become aware of the fact that it is me in the red cloak.

There was no doubt in her mind; she was going to Jerusalem again.

Fifty-six

March 1962
BRUSSELS/ANTWERP, BELGIUM

Haskel Zollman, first cousin to Alicja's maternal grand-father, warmly greeted Alicja when she arrived in Brussels. He and his wife went about showing their wide-eyed visitor the highlights of Belgium's capital city—the Place du Musée, the gothic Brussels Town Tower, and the Maison du Roi. Haskel Zollman and his family were secular, cosmopolitan Jews, and without the presumed religious expectations of the Barterers and Twerskys, Alicja's first days in Brussels felt liberating, as if she was released from under the lens of a microscope.

Now Alicja began to worry about what awaited her in New York. Aunt Shoshana's admonitions had been gentle but clear: her life with them would be tightly regulated. She pondered staying with the Zollmans for awhile and enjoying her newfound freedom.

"I'm afraid of what my life will be like in New York," Alicja confessed to Haskel Zollman's wife, Elana, one morning. "I don't know about this Bais Yaakov they'll send me to."

Alicja had let her guard down—a rare occurrence. And she did not immediately sense the change in Elana's demeanor. At dinner that evening, she expected the usual lively conversation and planning for the weekend. But no plans were discussed at dinner. After their children had gone to bed, Haskal and Elana called out for Alicja to join them in the den.

"We're sorry to tell you this," Haskal said softly. "But we need to travel and will be away for several weeks. I'm afraid you'll have to continue on your journey to New York."

Alicja was stunned. Haskal did not say where they were going, and Alicja sensed that she was not invited to ask. So she retreated to the guest room and began packing her belongings, her sense of liberation short-lived.

But Alicja was not ready to go to New York just yet. She contacted the Reich family in Antwerp before leaving Israel with a vague notion of visiting them while she was in Belgium —she'd learned that Isaac Reich had known her mother before the war— but the abrupt departure from the Zollman home had forced her hand. She either had to go to New York at once or delay her trip a bit longer and call on the Reichs. With hopes of being able to see Genowefa and Franciszek again, she decided to go to Antwerp.

Arriving in Anwerp by train, Alicja cast her eyes on the two figures that greeted her at the station. Rivka Reich, wearing a long print skirt and white blouse, stood beside her husband, Isaac, who wore the traditional garb of Hasidic Jews: a long black coat, wool fringes, and a black top hat. Alicja felt a strange sense of being judged as the Reichs helped her gather her luggage, as if she was a package they intended to examine before opening its contents. She wondered if she'd made a mistake by coming to them. Meeting Rivka's gaze, Alicja quickly shook off her angst and projected her best, most convincing smile, one meant to assure Rivka that she would be a most gracious visitor. From the station, Isaac led his wife and Alicja to his car, and from there he drove towards his home on the outskirts of the city.

In the car, Rivka briefly relayed to Alicja what her husband had told her about her mother, Adele. He was much older than she was, so he did not know her that well, but he recalled what a fine family she was part of. Alicja nodded tentatively, as if the threads that tied her to her family and heritage were still not completely stitched. Or perhaps she just found herself instantly uncomfortable with the Reichs. With the car pulling up to their home, it didn't much matter now. She just had to make the best of it.

She arrived on a Friday, just as she had when she first met the Barterers in Israel. By this time, she was familiar with many of the preparations needed for the arrival of the Sabbath later in the day, so the urgency she sensed as soon as they entered the home was not unexpected.

But Rivka assumed nothing. In quick order, she directed Alicja through a series of rules and tasks that had to be followed. She explained that the use of electricity on Shabbat was prohibited, as was cooking, sewing, or bathing. Rivka then led her to the bathroom, taking a roll of toilet paper and presenting it to Alicja.

"Take this roll and tear it up into individual squares," Rivka instructed. In response to Alicia's bewildered expression, she explained, "We are also not allowed to tear anything on Shabbat."

The Reichs appeared to be more observant than the Barterers, and Alicia soon found herself irked by the numerous regulations that were presented to her even after Shabbat was over. Still, she wanted to stay in Belgium a bit longer, if only to have the chance to see Genowefa and Franciszek again.

One afternoon as Alicja sat in the Reichs' den, she became aware of Isaac Reich's eyes measuring her. Rivka had left the house for an errand an hour earlier. Issac was a pious man; his interactions with Alicja had been limited while his wife schooled her in *halacha*, Jewish law. Suddenly aware of her aloneness with him, she rose from the couch and walked out the front door. Not again, she mumbled to herself.

Not long after, Alicja overheard Rivka conferring with Isaac about her.

"A twenty-two-year-old woman should not be single," Rivka emphatically declared. "Kirk would be a wonderful match for Alicja."

Kirk, a young man who worked with Isaac in the diamond exchange, was not a part of their Hasidic community. Word from neighbors was that Kirk's father had long ago abandoned religious observance, keeping a fabric store open on Shabbat and eating trief, not kosher, foods. But Rivka prided herself on not being judgmental like her neighbors. She would not judge Kirk because his parents had fallen off the *derech*, the path. He seemed nice enough, and he was hard-working and neatly dressed. So the Reichs arranged for him to meet Alicja.

Alicja found it curious that Rivka Reich wanted to introduce her to a non-observant man. Rivka, surprised when Alicja asked her about it, said of course she hadn't considered an observant man. "Who would want a wife who was raised in church and who had lived her entire life among the goyim?"

On the following Shabbat afternoon, while the Reichs napped in their bedroom, Alicja sat at the dining room table pondering her future. If she could only go home. She'd reconciled with Franciszek, and Genowefa surely needed her. How wonderful it would be to see them, to embrace them again, to be in the familiar, comforting surroundings of home.

She took a pen and pad of paper from the credenza and began writing the Swiateks a letter. Scribbling furiously, Alicja didn't notice Isaac emerge from the bedroom. When he saw what she was doing, his face reddened and his expression grew stern.

"What are you doing?" he scolded.

Alicja looked up, startled.

"I repeat—what are you doing?"

Alicja trembled like a child.

"It is forbidden to write on Shabbat. Why do you commit such an affront in our home?" Isaac collected himself for a moment, as if he was considering what punishment to administer. "Perhaps," he huffed, "I should tell the Twerskys the kind of girl they are bringing to New York."

Alicja, unable to find words to respond, grabbed the notepad and retreated to her bedroom.

Alicja sent the letter to her parents on Monday. A return letter arrived a little over a week later. She took it into her room, tore it open in haste and began reading. It was written in Franciszek's precise, perfect script, probably with his favorite black ink fountain pen.

> *Our Dearest Ala,*
>
> *Your mother and I miss you very much, and not a day goes by when we don't think of you. But as much as we miss you, we do not think you should come home. There is nothing to come home to. There is nothing for you here. You chose a new road for yourself and now you must follow it. I know you will face obstacles along the way, but you must overcome them. We will visit you when you are settled. May God be with you, Ala.*
>
> *Love,*
>
> *Papa and Mama*

Alicja could hardly believe what she had just read. Her heart sank as she read it again. She crumpled the letter slowly in her hands. How could they be so cruel? How could they abandon her in this time of need? Now it seemed she had no one to turn to. No one in the entire world.

Alicja continued to see Kirk. She enjoyed his company, but

had little interest in deepening their relationship. She casually mentioned her friendship with Kirk in a letter to Shoshana.

Shoshana Twersky's reply was not casual. She expressed stern disapproval that Alicja was passing the time with a secular Belgian man. And she was incensed that the Reichs had introduced her to such a man. Only a man from the finest Orthodox family would do for her Alicja!

Alicja had delayed her trip to them long enough, Shoshana concluded. She must leave for New York within the next forty-eight hours or the invitation would be withdrawn.

Shoshana's stern letter came as a surprise and a relief; it seemed to resolve Alicja's predicament. Two days later, on an early morning in June 1962, Alicja boarded a Pan American jet bound for New York. She settled into a seat by the window and the plane ascended into the Belgian sky. As she beheld her last views of Europe she imagined the Reichs returning to their Hasidic world in Antwerp, the Zollmans living richly and freely in Brussels, the Barterers secure in their Petach Tikva enclave, Franciszek on a commuter train headed to Krakow, and Genowefa cleaning the breakfast dishes in Bochnia.

Somewhere over the Atlantic Ocean, Alicja closed the window shade, leaned her seat back, and sank into a long, deep sleep.

Fifty-seven

October 2008
JERUSALEM, ISRAEL

As Lucia considered her plans for her next trip to Jerusalem, Lisa surprised her with some plans of her own. Following an earlier wedding in Boston to Howard Edelstein, himself a child of a Holocaust survivor, Lisa wanted an additional ceremony in Israel, one infused with the sense of spirituality unique to the Holy Land. Lucia was thrilled to be able to celebrate with Lisa and Howard while at the same time follow her own mission.

Lucia once again stood in the plaza facing the Western Wall. Fourteen years earlier, she had approached the Western Wall in anger, despondent at having been "orphaned" for the third time—losing her parents, losing the Swiateks, and mourning her husband. With a sense that she had been touched by the Divine, she left the Wall comforted in the belief that she would be cared for, that she'd find companionship, that she would not be alone anymore. Now as she again stood in the shadow of the Wall, she pondered a promise unrealized—she was still alone; there was no man in her life. Yet she also knew she was not truly alone: the Divine essence was with her.

"I brought You the fruits of my work, as You asked," she whispered, clutching the copy of the writings she brought with her, with no clear reason why she had been directed to do so. She looked upward and waited. Then she wept, an involuntary, reluctant sob. Before she could contemplate what to do next, she sensed the Divine voice entering her consciousness.

Wipe your tears. There is no need to cry. Your work will help re-build the Temple.

Lucia felt a shock. *The Temple*? She expected some Divine acknowledgment that her long journey was nearing an end. Yet the message she received indicated it was not. Then there was the matter of the substance of the message: what she was she supposed to do about it?

She glanced down at the manuscript in her hands and con-templated a fresh question. The Temple was destroyed over two thousand years ago. *Why* hadn't it been rebuilt? And just how was *she* supposed to help rebuild it?

She waited for a sign, some indication of what she was sup-posed to do next. Nothing happened. When she felt a drop of rain on her shoulder, she looked up at the darkening sky, hailed a taxi, and climbed inside just it began to pour.

"It's the first rain of the season," the cab driver said as he drove her through the streets of Jerusalem to her hotel. She'd arrived in time for Sukkot, a harvest festival. A prayer for rain, Tefillat Geshem, is traditionally recited on the first day of the seven-day festival, beseeching God's blessings for a good harvest.

Lucia made it to her hotel room just before the beginning of Shabbat and lit the Sabbath candles. The next day, she walked to the Yemin Moshe Synagogue, which she heard held a spirited service. She walked up a narrow set of stairs to the women's sec-tion, a small balcony with four rows of chairs. She sat in the first row and surveyed the ornate sanctuary below her, impressed with its beauty. She rose up from her seat with the rest of the congregation when the ark was opened and a Torah was removed amidst a rising chorus of song and prayer. An image located just above the ark caught her eye. She hadn't noticed it earlier.

It was a painting of a golden eagle.

Fifty-eight

June 1962
LONG BEACH, NY

Alicja had barely stepped off the plane when she heard Shoshana Twersky shouting, "Lusia! Lusia!"

Shoshana rushed up and embraced her with a force that nearly toppled her. Shoshana's four sons, Alexander, Haim, David, and Simon, looked on with bemusement. Abraham smiled warmly. They waited patiently for the women to separate before greeting and welcoming "Lusia," a new name fused from previous nicknames.

Alicja had noted the change when she first received the student visa from Shoshana, that her name was listed as "Lusia Zollman," not Alicja Swiatek. She had considered asking Shoshana how and why her name was changed, and why it was changed to Lusia Zollman (her mother's maiden name) as opposed to her birth name (Rose Berl), but she decided against it; perhaps the fewer questions, the better. Besides, all that mattered was getting to New York, regardless of what name anyone called her. And now she was here!

Shoshana and Abraham Twersky had managed to flee from their hometown in Poland at the onset of German invasion. They landed in Siberia, a miserable frozen tundra that nonetheless proved to be preferable to the concentration camps of occupied

Poland. After surviving the war with their family relatively intact, they immigrated to the United States in the early 1950s via various stops in Europe.

Abraham Twersky was an astute businessman. The family eventually found success in New York, where he supported a number of philanthropic endeavors—contributing to local charities, restoring Jewish cemeteries and synagogues in Eastern Europe, and in one instance of benevolence, sending care packages to a distant cousin and her adoptive parents in Bochnia, Poland.

Lusia spent her first few weeks in New York accompanying Shoshana on her various errands and charitable organization obligations. For the first time in her life, she felt truly safe and secure. And Shoshana made her feel like she was home. She began Judaic lessons to continue the education she started in Israel and Belgium. Shoshana also took her to clothing and cosmetics stores and bought her a new wardrobe. Much like the silver Shabbat candles resting on the credenza, Lusia was to be polished for presentation and integration into their close-knit religious community.

Lusia was also introduced to a Jewish girl named Miriam who had arrived in Brooklyn from Poland a year earlier. Like Lusia, she had been raised in a Catholic home. The two quickly formed a close friendship. They attended classes in Judaism together, enjoyed movies, and window shopped along Madison Avenue.

Miriam was charismatic, and was seemingly adjusting well to her new surroundings. A successful businessman from Detroit she'd met several months earlier was courting her intently. Lusia found Miriam's company appealing, even elevating. Miriam was the embodiment of a future that held much promise yet was deeply rooted in an inescapable past. Not since her friendship with Marysia had she bonded with a peer the way she did with Miriam. She looked forward to spending the rest of summer with her.

One morning, Shoshana's eldest son, Alexander, and his wife, Sophie, arrived to take Lusia for what they promised would be a meaningful trip to Brooklyn's Boro Park. Lusia sat nervously in the back seat with Sophie while Alexander navigated the pothole-scarred streets.

Alexander parked the car in front of a modest-looking brownstone and asked Lusia to accompany him inside. To Lucia's surprise, Sophie said she would remain in the car. Alexander escorted Lusia up the brownstone steps. The door easily opened with a slight turn of the brass doorknob. Alexander led Lusia through a dimly lit foyer and down a series of small steps into a narrow hallway. The faint smell of leftover lunch—some kind of fish—hung in the air.

A doorway to the left of a small, open kitchen was slightly ajar. Alexander pushed it open and walked into the room without as much as a "hello" or a knock. A man with a long, greying beard in a somewhat ruffled white shirt sat hunched over a desk with a Bible or some other religious text opened out before him. He removed his reading glasses and looked up affectionately at Lusia. She thought it strange, since she had never seen him before. Outwardly similar to the many Hasidic men she had observed in Israel and Belgium, she instinctively knew this man was very different.

The man said something in Yiddish to Alexander, motioning the two of them to be seated on a set of pinewood chairs across from his desk.

"This is the Bobover Rav," Alexander whispered. "Rabbi Solomon Halberstam, one of the foremost rabbinical giants in the world."

Halberstam was the third Bobover Rebbe. He succeeded his father, Ben Zion, who had been murdered by the Nazis in 1941.

After the war, he had come to New York with the remnants of the Hassidic group and was rebuilding the movement.

"The rabbi was in the Bochnia ghetto at the same time your parents were there," Alexander said. "He remembers meeting them. He remembers urging them to try a second time to give you away to a Christian home for safekeeping, even though they had been betrayed once."

Lusia sat stunned, unable to speak. Even though she sensed that the silence was making Alexander uncomfortable, she didn't know what she should say.

"I am sorry, Lusia," Alexander said, breaking the silence. "Perhaps it was too soon. I didn't think. . .I can't imagine how this must be for you...I should not have. . ."

The Bobover Rav interjected, speaking to Alexander in Yiddish while gently glancing at Lusia.

"The Rav says that your parents were wonderful, brave people," Alexander translated. "In the short time he knew them they earned his utmost respect. How sorry he is for your loss. He has pledged to say Kaddish for them." Lusia's eyes grew moist, but she tightened her jaw and held back her tears.

"He also says he is overjoyed and fortunate to see you here before him. He wishes to bestow a special blessing upon you. He wishes to bless you for a new life."

Lusia felt she hardly had time to contemplate her old life. Her head bowed as she felt the pain of all the difficult choices she'd been forced to make these past few years, of all that she had given up and left behind. Seeing the rabbi sitting across from her, she wondered why her parents could not have escaped with him.

"*Es zee gezunt?*" the Bobover Rav asked Alexander, the expression of concern on his face needed no translation.

Lusia lifted her head and nodded. She felt comforted in the rabbi's presence. He had looked into her parents' eyes, extracted their prayers for her, and absorbed them into his own essence. Suddenly hearing his prayers meant more than anything else in her life.

"Solst zein gebentcht," he began softly. *May you be blessed.*

Lusia took in the Rebbe's words. The rabbi's study was musty, with hundreds of volumes crowding the open bookshelves. But Lusia felt a fresh, gentle breeze wafting through the room, carrying the spirit of the heavens.

Lusia's Judaic tutoring was going well, but Alexander and Sophie thought it was not enough. Lusia was learning the rules but missing the rhythms and flavors of Jewish life—the dress, mannerisms, talk, and peer interaction—that a *frum*, or religious girl, would have soaked up since childhood.

Then Sophie had an idea for how to go about filling in these missing pieces: send Lusia to a summer camp established for the girls of Brooklyn's Bobov community. Alexander heartily agreed. It was summer, after all, an ideal time to catch Lusia up before Rosh Hashanah and the High Holidays in the fall. No doubt the New Year would bring her a most wonderful match. Arrangements were swiftly made.

Nestled in New York's Catskill Mountains, Camp Gila boasted lush greenery, a girls-only swimming pool, and a sanctuary for prayer and study. Alexander and Sophie dropped Lusia off at camp, certain that Lusia would emerge at summer's end as a frum girl with a most promising future.

But at twenty-two, Lusia was several years older than the oldest counselors at Camp Gila, and much older than the girls who had flocked to the camp since they were in grade school. Most expected to be long married by Lusia's age—by twenty at very latest.

Already an anomaly and a curiosity at Camp Gila, word spread that she had been personally blessed by the Bobover Rav, engendering a sort of reverence. One camper dashed to retrieve a prayer book for her during services; another demonstrated the proper way to wash one's hands and recite the appropriate blessing before eating.

These were among the patterns of observant life the Twerskys hoped Lusia would absorb, but as the days passed the lessons seemed to elude rather than engage her. The girls of Camp Gila—the Rivkas, Chayas, and Sarahs—had grown up sharing traditional stories and songs. Their aspirations rarely ventured beyond the confines of their *eruv*. Even their clothes on the hot, steamy summer days—long-sleeved blouses and skirts resting well below their knees—seemed to have been manufactured from the same sheet of fabric. These girls were unlike any Lusia had encountered before, just as she was unlike anyone they'd encountered.

At night, Lusia lay somberly in her cabin bed, pondering her future. She had so wanted to be a part of the Twersky family. She had embraced the Bobover Rav's blessing. But the demands of living a strictly observant lifestyle were too much. In Israel and in Belgium, and in her first weeks with the Twerskys, she was only an observer. She was Alicja Swiatek, learning about the many rituals and traditions of the people of her birth. At the Bobover camp, the expectation was that she would stop being an observer and become an observant Jew.

She was raised in a Catholic culture steeped in rules and rituals. But those rules and rituals often felt more intrusive than spiritual, like a barrier suppressing the communication she wanted to have directly with God. Now she felt the same about the numerous Jewish laws and rituals. Yet she dared not express such thoughts and feelings to anyone, certainly not to the Twerskys. Her days at Camp Gila became longer, and her blessed new life hardly seemed to be a blessing at all.

A phone call from her friend Miriam interrupted what might have been another pensive evening for Lusia. Miriam was staying at a less observant camp nearby. Miriam called Lusia several times during the week and, hearing the unhappiness in her voice, urged her to come to visit her camp. Lusia declined, citing her obligation to the Twerskys. Lusia was happy and relieved when Miriam offered to come visit her at Camp Gila.

The girls of Camp Gila looked on with a mixture of curiosity and amusement as Miriam made her way to the main building to meet her friend Lusia. The dark-haired girl walked across the campgrounds carrying a long-necked black guitar case, wearing a pink cotton dress with white sandals.

That evening, Miriam removed her guitar from the case, placed two wooden stools for her and Lusia to sit on, and performed a medley of songs familiar to the camp girls and staff. With the audience in the palm of her hand, she asked Lusia to join her in song as they launched into Polish folk melodies that at first startled and then enthralled the gathering.

"The two of you are a breath of fresh air," one of the counselors whispered to Miriam and Lusia as they walked towards Lusia's cabin.

The campers of Camp Gila looked forward to more performances, but Miriam had other plans. She learned that a man she knew from Detroit, a friend of her boyfriend, would be coming to the nearby Concord Hotel over the weekend. The man's name was Herman Weitzman. Miriam wanted Lusia to come with her and meet him.

"I'll find a way for the two of us to slip out of here for a few hours on Sunday," she told Lusia. "And I have the perfect dress for you to wear."

Spread over two thousand scenic acres along Kiamesha Lake

in the heart of the Catskill Mountains is an area known as the Borsht Belt. Its summer resorts served as a social hub for Jewish communities stretching from nearby New York to as far away as Detroit and launched the careers of some of America's most famous entertainers.

At the Concord Hotel, men in golf shirts milled about the hallways, gathering clubs, partners, and tee time slips. Families with young children escaped the pounding heat with a dip at the Olympic-size swimming pool. And in the atrium outside the main dining hall, Miriam and Lusia awaited a meeting with Herman Weitzman, who'd traveled from Detroit. With Miriam's guidance, Lusia had prepared meticulously for this moment. She wore a beige cashmere sweater with a mink trim collar overlaying a sleeveless black dress. Finally, Herman appeared—about a half-hour late.

"Lusia, I'd like you to meet Herman Weitzman, " Miriam said.

Lusia lifted her eyes to meet Herman's, and she was struck by something about him that she liked. Yet she quickly braced for disappointment, noticing that he had taken inventory of her and retreated a step or two back.

"Nice meeting you," he mumbled, then turned and walked away.

"I'm sorry," Miriam said. "I don't know what happened."

The two friends left the Concord holding hands. Just before climbing into the taxi idling at the lobby entrance, Lusia turned back to take a last look at the façade of the grand hotel and sighed.

Fifty-nine

August 2009
NEW YORK, NY

Nearly one year after her trip to bring the "fruits of her work" to Jerusalem, Lucia's question about the Temple remained unanswered: what did *"your work will help rebuild the Temple"* mean?

Once again, her dreams offered a clue. In one dream she was standing at the peak of a mountain, yet was denied the opportunity to "see the other side." Suddenly, she *and* the mountain shifted. In the next part of the dream, she was on the ground of an old structure that resembled a temple or monastery. A man wearing a cloak approached her. She asked whether she could go back up the mountain; she wanted to try again to "see the other side." The man in the cloak said she could not.

Engrossed in trying to understand the dream and decipher the identity of the man in the cloak, Lucia closed her eyes, meditated, and asked for answers.

A man, who she guessed to be some sort of holy figure appeared to Lucia in her dream that night. He was helping her serve food to a celebratory gathering of young people in their twenties or early thirties. The man walked over to a set of double doors and proceeded to open them. A pristine, sun-drenched beach appeared before them—ocean waves crashing majestically over the sand.

Upon awakening from her dream, Lucia placed her journal in her lap and began to write. Again these were not words she consciously composed. The words seemed to enter her essence and flow through her pen.

The mountain that I have shown you is a temple not of stones, but of love. It is a temple of light that you carry in your heart.

Lucia relaxed her grip on the pen. How could she rebuild a temple made of stones, anyway? Yet the words piqued her curiosity about the dream of the mountain from whose peak she could not see "the other side;" the mountain that shifted along with her. She now wondered: how could her work help to rebuild a temple of *love*?

More clues, no doubt, would come.

Sixty

August 1962
LONG BEACH, NY

Miriam left New York to be closer to her Detroit boyfriend, Fred Ferber, leaving Lusia to contemplate how she would cope with the rest of summer at Camp Gila. After one more day, Lusia decided she could not cope. But what could she do? She didn't want to disappoint Alexander and Sophie, not to mention Shoshana and Abraham. Yet she couldn't stay either.

She packed her bags and took a bus back to Long Beach. But rather than go back to Shoshana, she walked to the home of Shoshana's youngest son, Simon, who'd been something of a confidante since she'd arrived in New York.

Lusia was leaning against the porch column when Simon and his wife arrived home. Surprised to see her there, Simon quipped, "Too much sun for your fair skin over there at Camp Gila?"

"I didn't see that much sun; I was too busy studying."

"Well, then. . . I'm surprised you didn't come here sooner."

Lusia chuckled, relieved that she'd made the right choice to come to Simon.

Simon allayed her fears about how others in the family would respond to her early exit from the camp. "Don't worry," he assured her. "I'll smooth things over with my parents and brothers."

Lusia was grateful. She briefly mentioned her experience at the Concord Hotel, and then asked for some paper and an envelope. She felt the need to write to Genowefa and Franciszek.

My Dearest Mama,

I hope you are well. I had a feeling from your last letter that not all is as well as you say. You probably don't want me to worry, so you don't tell me everything. But I worry anyway. I don't stop thinking about you. How I wish I could see you, for even a minute.

My emotions are so crazy, Mama. I don't know how to begin. The Twerskys are wonderful to me, so you need not be concerned. But I'm confused. I was at the camp they sent me to, but it was challenging. My friend Miriam came to see me there and made it fun. But now she is engaged to be married and will be moving to Detroit. The Twerskys make me feel at home. But I can't help feeling confused.

Mama, there is this man Miriam introduced me to. I saw him for only a moment, but I can't stop thinking about him. I don't know why. I don't think he was interested in me, though. One of Aunt Shoshana's daughters-in-law said that a girl my age had better be married soon or it will be very hard to find a man who would want me. I wish I could talk to you, Mama. Love to Papa.

All My Love,

Your Ala

Herman Weitzman, or Heinuch as he was then called, was born to a well-to-do, religious family in Kielce, Poland, in 1925. His parents, younger sister Paula, and dozens of aunts and uncles lived in a courtyard complex. At the outset of the German invasion in September 1939, his family fled east towards the Russian border, eventually settling in the Ukrainian town of Tulchin. Herman's mother returned alone to Kielce to retrieve family belongings and was detained there when the borders unexpectedly closed.

On Yom Kippur in 1942, some Jews in Tulchin prayed for Divine intervention as Nazi-supervised Ukrainian collaborators dug graves around the perimeter of their makeshift synagogue. Others prepared to resist: when the Nazi's attacked they'd mount a blockade at the ghetto walls and set the buildings ablaze, hoping the diversion would allow others to escape through openings in the walls into the surrounding forests.

On the night of September 23rd, seventeen-year-old Herman was startled awake by pandemonium. People shouted and rushed about as fires rapidly consumed the ghetto. He instinctively followed a throng of escaping Jews into the forest. When Herman finally paused to catch his breath, he realized his father and sister were not with him. He would never see them or his mother again.

Alone in the forests for months, he eventually joined several partisan units, some Jewish and some Russian. There were harrowingly close calls—he was nearly axed by a Ukrainian farmer who found him sleeping in his barn, and then he was nearly shot to death by a fellow Russian partisan who hated Jews as much as he hated the Nazis. Finally he was "liberated" by the Russians and conscripted into the Red Army, where he remained until well after the war ended.

He slipped out of his Red Army uniform in the summer of 1946 and made his way back home to Kielce, hoping to find his family. Dejected at finding no one, he left Kielce on July 1, 1946, three days before a pogrom there took more Jewish lives.

From Kielce, Herman migrated to Germany where some relatives had settled. Most of them soon moved on to Israel, Canada, and the United States, but Herman remained behind for the better part of a decade. He'd had enough fighting and wanted no more of it in Israel. America was a land of opportunity, yet Herman had no desire to plan or work for the future. He wanted only to live for the moment, and he got by through odd jobs and selling American goods in postwar Germany.

When the last of his relatives moved to the then burgeoning city of Detroit, Herman, now approaching his thirties, followed them. He worked at a series of jobs at Ford and other companies. Then he and a partner established a wholesale clothing business.

The business was modestly successful, and Herman had made friends within Detroit's close-knit survivor community. But he did not feel rooted to anything or anyone, and wasn't sure, after all he had lost, that he'd ever want to.

Rugged and handsome, he was at first a sought-after bachelor. But he soon developed a reputation as a ladies' man who had little interest in commitment.

Herman Weitzman's abrupt rejection of Lusia after their brief, awkward meeting had seemed final. So Miriam was surprised when Lusia contacted her saying she wanted to see Herman again.

Herman traveled to New York every month to meet with clothing manufacturer representatives, so Miriam and Fred, who was now her fiancé, passed on Lucia's request to Herman. Herman had given little thought to the girl he had met at the Concord Hotel who'd been wearing a ridiculous cashmere sweater with a mink trim collar on a blazing hot summer day. Too much to handle, he thought at the time. Yet to his surprise, he agreed to meet her on his next visit to New York.

The Twerskys demanded that any meeting take place in the company of their extended family. Herman spent the Sabbath with them in Long Beach. Asked to lead parts of the prayer service and offer a few words of D'var Torah, Herman strained but somehow retrieved memories of both from his childhood days in *cheder*. Lusia was impressed, and hoped the Twerskys were as well.

When Shabbat ended, Sophie escorted Lusia and Herman on a walk along the beach. Herman didn't say much about himself, but when he did speak, he struck Lusia as a man of depth, versed in his own heritage, knowledgeable about politics and the arts, and soulful in a way she could not explain. Herman found Lucia attractive, shy, and unpretentious.

He wasn't sure if he had passed the Twerskys' test, but he hoped to see Lusia again on his next trip to New York. And Lusia hoped to see him.

That August, Lusia traveled to Detroit for Miriam's wedding shower. She planned on staying for a few days and looked forward to seeing Herman, with whom she was now corresponding regularly. At the shower, she mentioned Herman to one of the guests. The woman growled in response.

"You're going to see Herman? I know all about him. I don't want to see an innocent girl like you taken advantage of."

Lusia was startled. Had she made a mistake? Should she still see him? She decided to keep her date with Herman but to prepare a plan. She would learn more about his family, his upbringing, his business, and his friendships. Then she would ascertain his intentions. If there was any hint of truth behind what the woman at the wedding shower had implied, she would let him have it.

Herman made meticulous plans for their date. Thinking that Lusia would be keeping the same observant standards as the Twersky family, he decided to take her to a café that served kosher food and greet her with a bow before asking whether he could take her hand, since touching between unmarried men and woman was prohibited in some Orthodox traditions. He washed and vacuumed his Buick, put on a navy blue blazer, and drove to the home of Miriam's aunt, who was hosting Lusia during her trip.

On arriving, Herman pressed the doorbell twice. Miriam's aunt answered it and summoned Lusia, who appeared moments later with a scowl on her face that surprised and jarred Herman.

Lucia had reviewed her plan and rehearsed the speech she intended to deliver to Herman later in the evening. But as she closed the door and faced him on the porch it all came pouring out.

"I've heard all about you," she said, her eyes burning into his. "I heard that you have been with many, many women, and that you have no intention of ever marrying."

Lusia did not wait for a response. "So, if you don't plan on marrying me, I will pack my bags this minute and return to New York."

Herman was speechless; he wasn't sure whether he should be roaring in laughter, aghast at her ridiculous ultimatum, or dumfounded by her innocent naïveté. The truth was, he had been given ultimatums before, but never like this, and never by a woman he found so irresistibly sincere, vulnerable, and beautiful.

"Just give me a chance," he said softly.

Lusia, appeased, gave him her hand, and together they drove off into the evening.

Over the next several weeks Lusia and Herman spoke on the phone and exchanged frequent letters. Herman's letters were poetic, funny, and sometimes obscure. One letter in particular confounded her; it spoke of an abyss, and of heaven, and of building bridges to protect them from falling. Perplexed, Lusia put the letter in a deep pocket of her purse and forgot it there.

Meanwhile, Miriam's wedding in New York in mid-September was fast approaching, and Herman and Lusia were both planning to attend.

Herman's business took him on the road throughout small towns in Michigan. In Bay City one of Herman's best customers, Lillian Murphy, owner of Lillian's Fashions, had become a trusted friend, confidant, and shoulder for Herman to lean on. Bay City was far from the pressures of Jewish community life in Detroit, and even further from the ghosts of Europe that still haunted Herman's dreams. Herman rarely opened up to anyone. But Lillian Murphy, a round, cheerful, Irish Catholic woman who valued church and family above all else, treated Herman like a son. And she was the one person he could talk to about Lusia now.

So on his next visit to Lillian's shop before the wedding, he told her about the Polish girl who had stirred feelings within him he'd thought would never emerge. Yet he was also agitated about it, unsure of that to do next.

"Herman, my boy," she said softly, resting her hand gently on his shoulder. "I've seen the emptiness in your heart. This girl sounds like someone special—a gift from God. Whatever you do, Herman, don't let her go."

Gathering her mothering instincts, she faced Herman squarely, looked him in the eye, and said, "Don't let her go. If you do, you need not come back here again."

After Miriam and Fred's wedding ceremony and reception, Herman escorted Lusia by taxi back to the Twerskys' home in Long Beach. He seemed pensive, but Lusia chose not to pry. As the taxi came to a stop in front of her home, Herman asked Lusia to wait a moment. He hardly spoke to her during the ride home, leaving her to wonder if she had done anything wrong.

"Lusia," he said in a whisper, "will you marry me?"

"Yes," she said without hesitation. "Yes."

Lusia shrieked with excitement when she announced the engagement to the Twerskys the next morning.

"Not so fast!" Alexander erupted.

The Twerskys had done some checking in Detroit, and they questioned whether Herman met the religious standards they envisioned for Lusia. Herman was at his hotel preparing to return to Detroit when he was summoned back to Long Beach.

In Abraham and Shoshana's living room, Herman found himself in the company of all four Twersky sons in addition to the family patriarch. Lusia was directed to join the women in the kitchen—all of the Twersky wives had also descended on the home—where bagels and lox spreads were being prepared.

The Twersky men, all dressed in dark suits, approached Herman casually, asking him about his business and how he enjoyed Miriam's wedding. Herman was about to relax when the men formed a semicircle in front of him.

It seemed to Herman that the *bet din*, the Jewish court, was again in session. The questions came fast and furious:

"Where do you daven?"

"With whom do you spend Shabbos?"

"What kind of yeshivot exist in Detroit?"

During the tribunal Lusia paced nervously in the kitchen. She very much wanted to marry Herman, but she was prepared to abide by the Twerskys' decree. Their hastily called summit left no doubt that Lusia was a much-loved member of their family. She trusted her fate and was relieved and comforted to have a strong family standing behind her.

After awhile, to her relief, laughter and the clang of schnapps glasses replaced the stern solemnity that began the proceedings. Herman had engaged the Twersky men with confidence and flair. He quoted from the Talmud. He spoke of his days at *cheder*.

Then he played his trump card: with a pride that startled even the grand patriarch, Herman announced that he was a direct descendant of the renowned teacher and scholar known as the Alexander Rov, Rabbi Hanoch of Alexander, who led the Polish Jewish community of Aleksandrów in the mid 1800s. He was, in other words, Jewish royalty. He had *yichus*.

With that revelation, lingering questions about Herman's suitability for Lusia dissolved. Now a wedding had to be planned. Shoshana set December 26th as the date, hoping arrangements could be made for the Swiateks to attend. But Franciszek had been diagnosed with leukemia, and Genowefa's heart condition had worsened. Neither would be able to travel.

Lusia was devastated. She cried in Shoshana's arms.

"They are always with you in your heart," Shoshana whispered. "And in ours too."

Feeling Shoshana's tears against her cheek, Lusia felt consoled, if only for the moment.

Herman Weitzman and Lusia Zollman were married on December 26, 1962, at Hirsch Hall on East Houston Street. The wedding was covered by the *Day Jewish Journal*, a local Yiddish newspaper, which deemed Lusia's background a story of interest.

Under the heading "A Dramatic Wedding," the article read:

> *The Hall was filled to capacity. Rabbis, Hasidim, women with sheitels, children, and the evening's hosts, the well-known Twersky family, were all there to rejoice at the wedding of a girl who remarkably had returned to her Jewish roots.*

> *The bride was shining with glowing radiance. Guests surrounded her from all sides wishing her mazel and long life. But nowhere in the crowd was her father, mother, grandparents, aunts, uncles, or old friends.*

It was a wedding to remember. Lusia was placed on the bridal throne to await Herman's arrival. The Twersky women, Miriam, and others danced and sang around her. She was radiant, a bright light at the center of raucous celebration of joy and love. Filled with emotion, she drew in deep breaths, inhaling the overwhelming beauty of the moment.

Herman Weitzman, the bridegroom, was born in Kielce, Poland. He lost his parents and sister in the war; a mere boy who had to face survival on his own.

Herman entered and was seated at the head of the chasen's tish, a long table laden with food and drink that served as the headquarters for the business and merriment of making a man a husband. A *ketubah* was placed before him, and the terms of the marriage contract were read by one of three rabbis the Twerskys had engaged.

As tradition dictated, Herman was presented with a kittel to wear to the *chuppah*. The white linen or cotton robe is a symbol of purity and a reminder of the solemnity of the day that bride and groom make a commitment to each other and to God. The same kittel is also worn as a shroud at death, a poignant message at a moment of joy to strive to pursue a life of meaning and value. Herman stretched his arms out as the Hasidic entourage placed the kittel upon him. Thinking his preparation complete, he stepped forward and was immediately pulled back. In the custom of some Hasidic sects, an overcoat was thrust over his kittel. He recoiled as the overcoat imprisoned one of his arms within its heavy fabric. This may be their custom, but it was not *his* family custom. He resented its imposition. Shoshana and Herman's aunt escorted Lusia in measured steps down the aisle toward a brightly decorated chuppah, where Herman awaited.

Lusia noticed a scowl on Herman's face; he seemed to be

struggling. She felt a wave of fear, realizing how little she knew this man fifteen years older than her. He was a mystery. Was he going to do something unexpected, run away from the chuppah or bring some embarrassment to Aunt Shoshana? Yet she had seen in him soulfulness with depth beyond her grasp. That was what had drawn her to him and what allowed her to trust him now.

Herman finally freed his arm from the kittel and overcoat. He saw Lusia standing before him, beautiful, her hopeful eyes concealing the grief, fears, and uncertainties they both felt. He too, sensing the depth of Lusia's soul, had pursued the brief courtship. For Herman it meant trying to throw off the weight of his past and overcome his trepidations about the future.

The rabbi read the sheva b'rachot, the traditional seven blessings. On the floor next to Herman lay a goblet wrapped in a thin white cloth. In a symbolic act in memory of the destruction of the Jerusalem Temple, Herman stomped on the glass, shattering it in pieces. A chorus of "mazel tov" and other cheers filled the hall.

The article in the *Day Jewish Journal* concluded:

The orchestra played; the guests danced joyously; and for two children of the Nazi hell, a new dawn with a bright horizon smiled upon them.

Sixty-one

The mountain that I have shown you is a temple not of stones, but of love. It is a temple of light that you carry in your heart.

— From Lucia's journal, August 2009

September 2009
NEW YORK, NY

L ucia had experienced the Divine presence at Mt. Kuchumaa near Rancho La Peurta; she'd been to the summit at Machu Picchu where her spirit reached into the heavens; and now she dreamed about a mountain with a temple in its base, and encountered a holy man or prophet of some sort. What did it all mean?

As she'd done before, she walked into a bookstore with only a vague notion of what she was looking for. One book on the shelf looked intriguing—*The Isaiah Effect: Decoding the Lost Science of Prayer and Prophesy* by Gregg Braden, a former computer systems designer who now writes on topics that bridge science and spirituality. As she flipped through the pages of the book, a chapter entitled "The Mystery of the Mountain" captured her attention. While standing in the aisle she began reading. It described how the prophet Isaiah had opened a door to a path that may forever change the attitudes of humankind. One particular passage leaped out at her. It reads, in part:

Isaiah outlines a form of behavior that allows us to escape the darkness that he has witnessed. He begins by referring to a mystical key through which the people of any generation may redirect the events that lie ahead in their probable future. The key is identified in his vision as a 'mountain.' The prophet tells of a time when, in the presence of a mountain, 'the veil that veils all peoples, the web that is woven over all nations,' will be destroyed.

A mystical key? Lucia shivered at the recollection of her dream of a gold key opening a bank vault. The words on the page seemed inflamed with power and relevance. The author continues to discuss the mountain metaphor:

In Hebrew, the word for Jerusalem is Yerushalayim. Here the definition becomes very clear: it means "vision of peace." At last the mysterious meaning of Isaiah's message becomes clear. Isaiah's mountain is not a physical place, but a reference to the power of peace. . . . In the presence of the vision of peace, the veil that veils all peoples, the web that is woven over all nations, will be destroyed.

She had been unveiled in the same dream sequence in which the gold key appeared!

Lucia recalled the mountain dream in which a holy man or prophet had opened a set of double doors to reveal a panoramic view of the beach and ocean. What did the opening doors really reveal? A new horizon? A new world?

"Like our times," Braden writes, "Isaiah's times were ones of both healing and destruction. But choices can be made to avoid future suffering. What Braden calls The Isaiah Effect stands for the proposition that we embody the collective power to choose which future we experience."

Lucia exhaled deeply. The message was profound. The dreams and writings that had engrossed her for well over a decade were coming into greater focus. She'd made choices throughout her life, from the way she handled the adversity

of her schoolgirl days to the decision to continue her pursuit of a spiritual journey that was, at times, overwhelming and frightening.

Yet there was more work to be done, and so many unanswered questions. Also still lurking in her subconscious was the question of God's presence during times of destruction.

Sixty-two

January 1963 - Summer 1981
SOUTHFIELD, MICHIGAN

After a honeymoon in Montreal, the newlyweds settled into a one-bedroom garden apartment on Greenfield Avenue, a mile or so north of the Detroit city line, in the booming suburb of Southfield. Several new strip malls had sprouted along the street, giving it an urban, walkable feel. But it wasn't New York, and with Herman spending the better part of the week on the road in small towns throughout Michigan, Lucia—she had changed the spelling of her first name at Herman's urging (he thought "Lucia" to be more sophisticated)—often found herself alone in their sparsely decorated apartment, pondering her future.

She wanted to build, to conquer her new Detroit community as she'd once conquered grade school and gymnazjum. She envisioned having a family of status and accomplishment.

Herman, she quickly realized, was not quite as ready to launch their new dawn and bright horizon as she was. He'd return home from sales trips recalling the sales he missed, not the orders he filled. If a business quarter had been profitable, he anticipated recession next quarter. He loved Lucia's sense of style, and her ambition evoked both his surprise and admiration; yet he resisted assuming any leadership position in synagogue, as she urged.

Early in her marriage, she saw his outsized anger at the pettiest of annoyances—a shirt coming back from the dry cleaner with a button missing could send him into a tirade. Yet she also felt his tenderness and generosity of spirit. He relished buying her the best he could afford. He allowed her to embrace Jewish practice at her own pace, affording her the leeway she felt she lacked in Belgium or with the Twerskys. He honored the Swiateks, writing to them regularly both before and after they were married. He was, in short, an enigma.

Alone again when he was on the road, she would pull out the letter he'd written her during their brief courtship—the letter that had left her mystified.

Lusienko:

I am still thinking of you after our phone call. Your pleasant disposition provoked me to write this letter. There was no one who had the power to raise me to heaven and throw me to the abyss. When I am in heaven, I am dreaming and longing for you. I want to share with you a bliss that has no boundary. When I am in the abyss, I want you with me to prove that all is not lost. The one who tasted fruits from heaven cannot live in the dark abyss. With that gift, you can only discover new heavens and I will build bridges to protect us from falling.

Yours,

Heniek

Rereading the letter again and again yielded no more insight than the first time she read it. What did he mean by "abyss"? As she'd done before, she shrugged her shoulders and returned the letter to her purse.

She also recalled learning of a letter he'd sent to the Swiateks shortly before their wedding. "I'm going to marry a wonderful girl," he declared in the letter, "one who will save my life."

And perhaps, she considered, she could save his life. She could diffuse his angst, heal his wounds, and show him that it was possible to rebuild. Part of him wanted the same things she did, even if he did not quite know how to go about it. She would show him the way. Wasn't that the reason had she left Bochnia in the first place?

Lucia would have less time devoted to saving Herman than she thought. Less than three months into their marriage, she learned she was pregnant. And on October 12, 1963, she gave birth to a baby boy. As Lucia received the bundle the nurse handed her, she cautiously looked around the delivery room, as if some-one might be lurking in a corner, ready to seize her baby at any moment. Until now, it seemed nothing had ever truly been hers: not her straw cot in Bochnia, not her homes in Israel, Belgium, or Long Beach. It took several days for her to accept that this child, her son Mitchell, was hers and would not be taken away.

A daughter, Lisa, was born a year later. Her family— a foun-dation—was taking shape. Yet the glow of new motherhood was jarred when a telegram arrived on February 13, 1965, telling her Franciszek had died. Instinctively, she packed her suitcase.

"You can't go to Poland," Herman said. "You are a fugitive. You will be arrested as soon as you step off the plane."

"I don't care." Lucia wept, imagining Genowefa, the mother she'd abandoned, alone.

In the end, she realized Herman was right. She could not go. Nine months later Alexander and Sophie Twersky traveled to Poland to continue their work restoring damaged gravesites and supporting local Jewish organizations. Lucia asked them to visit Genowefa in Bochnia.

"You are a special woman," Alexander told Genowefa at their meeting in her home. "Not only for saving a little Jewish girl, but for raising a woman of great character and integrity. It is obvious how much love and wisdom she gleaned from this house."

"And you have been wonderful to my Ala," Genowefa responded. "As lonely as I have been since she left, I was always comforted that she was with a family that was good to her."

Lucia eagerly awaited word from Alexander and Sophie about their visit with Genowefa. But a different telegram from Poland arrived. Genowefa had died the morning after the Twersky's visit. No explanation of her death was given, but Lucia knew: Genowefa died of a broken heart.

Herman glanced at the telegram and grimaced. He never had the chance to say good-bye to his own mother, and he had helplessly searched for her long after the war ended, to no avail. He put on his overcoat and headed for the car.

"Where are you going?" Lucia asked.

"To play cards."

Lucia sat on the couch and gazed at a grainy television screen. She had a child wrapped up in each arm, yet she felt as alone as she'd ever been. She chewed deliberately on some breadsticks, waited for Mitchell and Lisa to fall asleep, and then allowed herself to cry. She mourned for Genowefa, and for her former life.

If Lucia never quite reached many of the goals she aspired to when she first got married and settled in Detroit, she still took pride and satisfaction at what had been accomplished. Herman was a warm, loving father. To build a solid Jewish foundation for Mitchell and Lisa, Herman and Lucia sent them to Akiva, an Orthodox Jewish day school. Mitchell and Lisa managed to balance the Orthodox teachings they learned at school with the traditional but not quite Orthodox lifestyle they had at home. Together with Miriam Ferber, her husband, Fred, and their three children, they formed an extended family sharing holiday traditions like Passover. With great *ruach*, or spirit, new life was infused into ancient Haggadah melodies and prayers that had been sung by their families in Poland for centuries before the war.

Years passed and the children grew older. Herman and Lucia planned a bar mitzvah for Mitchell in Israel. In December 1976, during Chanukah, Mitchell read from the Torah at the Western Wall in the presence of the Twerskys, the Barterers, and other relatives. At a reception following the service, Herman spoke to the gathering about the relationship of the bar mitzvah to Chanukah, which commemorates the Jewish victory over the Greeks and reclamation of the Temple.

"The war between the Greeks and the Jews was an ideological one," he said. "For the Greeks, beauty was external, while for Jews, it was their internal being that was most important. Our goal in life is to reach the highest possible spiritual level."

Herman turned his attention directly to Mitchell. "As the Maccabees lit the fires of the Jews' souls, so too have your parents, relatives, and these honored guests here today lit the fire of your soul so that this day may be the beginning of your climb to a high level of spirituality, happiness, and prosperity."

Lucia's face was flushed with pride. It was a moment of triumph.

In the years after the bar mitzvah, Lucia and Herman expanded their social circle, traveled, and explored new business opportunities.

But in the summer of 1981 things took a turn for the worse when Herman underwent heart surgery complicated by a postoperative infection. It would be months before he returned to work. When he did, he faced a confrontation with his longtime business partner, who sought to force Herman out and offered to buy his share of the partnership. Herman flatly refused. But he did not leave it at that. Lucia urged Herman to negotiate terms with his partner, to preserve value that had accumulated over the course of twenty-five years. Instead, bruised and feeling betrayed, Herman set out to destroy the business he had built up from scratch, to strip it down to its foundations. And he did it quickly. Employees were let go. Inventory was sold at cost. Equipment, furniture, and supplies were dismantled, sold, or trashed. The business warehouse, which sat on an increasingly valuable parcel of land in Bloomfield Hills, was sold at a fraction of its market value. The prominent sign on the front of the warehouse was finally removed and shredded. The business ceased to exist.

Home was next his next target. He'd long complained about Detroit as a place where no one understood him. Now Detroit had to go too. Again Lucia pleaded with him to preserve the lives they'd built over the course of their marriage. But like the business, the house was sold below market value. Prized belongings were sold or given away. Herman rented a U-Haul trailer and hitched it to their car.

The plan was to go to New York, where Mitchell and Lisa were already attending New York University. There Herman hoped to join the Twerskys in business.

Lucia felt more ambivalent than excited about new opportunities—she could not see Herman, used to being his own boss, working for someone else, even if they were her beloved relatives. Herman disregarded her concerns.

As night fell, the last package was squeezed into the U-Haul. Herman started the car and bolted for the highway. They did not say good-bye to their neighbors, acquaintances, or friends. They said good-bye to no one.

On the road to New York, Lucia sat in the passenger seat staring out into the surrounding darkness. With Herman's stress level palpably elevated, she feared for his health. She feared for her own safety. And she worried about the future.

Sixty-three

March 2010
NEW YORK, NY

At first Lucia thought her blurred vision might be due to allergies, a lingering virus, or perhaps she just needed a new set of eyeglasses. But her ophthalmologist had a different diagnosis: macular degeneration, a condition that gradually destroys the macula, the part of the eye that provides sharp, central vision needed for seeing objects clearly. Eventually, the ophthalmologist told her, she could lose nearly all of her sight. She left the doctor's office with a sense of doom.

Why her vision? Of all things, why must God take *that* from her? She had grown so much though her writing, through her *visions*. How did God expect her to continue her work to rebuild the temple if she could not see?

Returning home, she saw her journal resting on the nightstand. How much longer would she be able to see it? How much longer would she able to write in it and read what she had written? She felt like crying. Tired and despondent, she crawled into bed.

She soon began undergoing monthly eye injections that contained the macular degeneration progression. The injections were painful, and each appointment stirred a sense of anger and bewilderment over her affliction. Yet at the same time that she bemoaned the possibility of her condition compromising her on-going spiritual journey, she could accept the fact that it was *part of her journey*. Her faith would allow her to overcome fears of blindness. She would rise above this challenge too. If her physical vision was threatened—and she believed she would not be blind—her inner vision would remain intact. Gradually her anger subsided and gave way to determination. After all she'd been through, she would not let this defeat her. She continued to write and meditate as before, now with even greater fervor.

Sixty-four

April 1993
HALLANDALE, FLORIDA

The business opportunity with the Twerskys fizzled, as Lucia had feared. Herman gradually settled into a restless retirement that saw him and Lucia shuttling between New York and Florida, and to and from hospitals for Herman's various ailments. Yet they also made new friends, decorated a lovely condominium in Hallandale, and enjoyed walks along the beach.

But as Passover approached in April 1993, Herman was contemplating the future of his children. Mitchell was still establishing himself professionally as a lawyer. Perhaps more troubling to Herman was that Lisa, approaching thirty, was not yet married. Lisa was flying into Florida the morning of Passover Eve; Mitchell would arrive later that afternoon.

Herman and Lucia sat at their kitchen table overlooking the Atlantic Ocean, nibbling on some apricot rugaluch. Suddenly Herman saw a strip of white light cut like a laser across their plates. He abruptly stood up and told Lucia what he'd seen. She looked at him quizzically.

"It wasn't just the white light," Herman explained. "In that moment, I saw my grandfather, and he told me that I should expect a joyous simcha."

Herman explained that he had seen a vision of the same grandfather nearly fifty years earlier, when he sat inside the smoke- filled bowels of a Soviet tank engaged in a fierce battle. "You will walk away from this," his grandfather had told Herman then. In the end, every other tank in his battalion was destroyed. Herman's tank was spared and he was able to walk away.

"What do you think your grandfather meant by expecting a simcha?" Lucia asked.

"It can only mean Lisa," Herman said. "Hasn't she been dating that investment banker? I think his name is Joseph. Maybe she'll surprise me and bring him here. I better go out and buy some schnapps."

Lisa arrived at the condominium with a large kosher-for-Passover chocolate cake in her hand, but without Joseph. She had ended the relationship several days earlier.

At the seder that evening, Lisa could not account for Herman's somber expression. Mitchell noticed it as well and assumed that his father was worried about him.

"Let's turn this gloom around," he implored his father. "It's Pesach. We're all together. And we'll all be alright."

Herman leaned forward in his chair.

"Lucia, what do you think about what Mitchell said?"

"I think he's right. We should have a joyous Pesach and pray for the best."

"Well, you do have a direct line to God. So if you feel that way, I'm with you."

"I don't know about that…"

"But you do," Mitchell interrupted.

"Let's just continue the seder," Lucia pleaded.

After recounting the Israelites' plight in Egypt, recalling their hasty liberation and exodus into the desert, and invoking the revelation of the Torah at Mount Sinai, all wrapped around a festive meal, the seder was completed with everyone in good spirits.

As they lay in their bedroom after the seder, Herman edged closer to Lucia and put his arm around her shoulder.

"You're going to have a lot of nachas from the children," he said.

"*Me*? Why not we?"

But Herman did not answer.

Sixty-five

August 2011
KRAKOW, POLAND

Mitchell and his wife, Beverly, decided to have their daughter, Paula, now thirteen-years-old, celebrate her Bat Mitzvah in Poland, a decision inspired by Paula herself. She had been close to her grandmother since early childhood, sharing stories, writing in journals together, and even learning some Polish along the way. And Lucia adored Paula's emerging sense of style, as well as her sensitivity and intuitiveness; she was much like Lucia had been at her age. Lucia would mark Paula's milestones—her second birthday, her first day at school—with recollections of her own childhood with the Swiateks. She too felt a strong bond with Paula. But she was reluctant to go back to Poland again. She'd had enough.

"*Prosze, Nana,*" Paula pleaded. Lucia eventually melted.

Bat mitzvah arrangements were made with the help of Krakow's resident rabbi. He chose the Tempel Synagogue from among several sanctuaries that operated part-time. Some, like the Remuh Synagogue centered in Krakow's traditional Jewish quarter and named for a sixteenth-century scholar, are tourist attractions. On their trip back to Poland in 2004, Lucia and Mitchell had visited a number of synagogues, but they had not been to the Tempel Synagogue. Still, Mitchell accepted the rabbi's choice and prepared to travel to Poland.

From a rented apartment a few blocks away from the main market square, Mitchell's wife and son, Beverly and Joshua, explored the narrow cobblestone streets and contemporary stores housed in centuries-old structures. Meanwhile, Mitchell, Lucia, and Paula headed towards Kazimierz, the old Jewish quarter, where they'd made plans to meet the Krakow rabbi to preview the Tempel Synagogue and rehearse the ceremony.

They walked by a passageway that led to Szeroka Street, the heart of Kazimierz. Here along a square the equivalent of a long city block, the Remuh and Old Synagogues bookended several kosher-style restaurants, a Jewish bookstore, and hotels. This was where Lucia and Mitchell had spent most of their time on their 2004 trip. But now they were walking past the square, onto unfamiliar streets. At least twice, they asked a passerby to point them in the right direction to get to the Tempel Synagogue.

Turning onto Miodowa Street, Lucia felt a strange sense of familiarity. A few blocks further, Lucia made a right turn into a small courtyard and faced the grand façade of an impressive, neo-renaissance structure.

Could it be? she wondered. The rabbi escorted Lucia, Mitchell, and Paula into the structure, not yet illuminated. Slivers of light shined through the stained glass windows and framed the dome-shaped ark. Lucia marveled at the sanctuary's beauty, a stronger sense of familiarity now moving up her spine.

"I'm sorry we can't go upstairs," the rabbi apologized. "The balcony is being renovated."

"The balcony?" Lucia spun towards her left and looked up at the balcony. "I can't believe it! This is it!"

"What is it?" The rabbi asked.

"This is where I was fifty years ago! This is the first syna-gogue I ever walked into. This is where I went when I left my parents on the morning of Rosh Hashanah and met the Lawaszes, the Jewish family from Krakow I'd been introduced to. This is where my road out of Poland started. . .where I began to return to my Jewish roots. I remember sitting in the women's section in a balcony. I remembered that the synagogue had a balcony."

Lucia paused to catch her breath.

"That's why none of the synagogues we went to in 2004 looked familiar," Mitchell said. "None of them had a balcony." Lucia nodded. "But I wonder why we couldn't find *this* synagogue," Mitchell asked. "It was only a few blocks away."

"Maybe I didn't want to find it," Lucia answered. "Maybe I wasn't ready. It's painful to remember. The train ride home, the choice I had to make. . .it led to my leaving my parents."

Mitchell threw his arms around his mother. Paula joined them.

"Who would believe that this is where we'll have Paula's Bat Mitzvah?" Lucia marveled. "Who would believe?"

The rabbi raised his arms in heavenly tribute.

At her bat mitzvah service, Paula spoke poignantly about the significance of her being in Poland, of remembering the trag-edies of the past, and about the rebirth of Jewish life now taking place there. A nearby kosher restaurant and a new Jewish Com-munity Center were evidence of openly Jewish culture re-emerg-ing in Krakow. Then Paula and Lucia together read a passage from Shir Hashirim, Solomon's Song of Songs.

I am a rose of Sharon, a lily of the valleys . . .

Afterwards, Mitchell addressed the congregants.

"Many people read Shir Hashirim as an allegory of God's love," he said, "while others find messages of the Shechina,

God's female essence, as an essential part of Divine unity. For my mother, whose birth name was Rose, there is yet another interpretation that has meaning for her. 'Sharon' also suggests an 'orbit of light,' with a rose at its center."

Lucia surveyed the crowd gathered in the synagogue. She was heartened by the sight of Olaf's family and other members of their *havurah* who had traveled from Warsaw to attend. She was happy to see her good friend and fellow child Holocaust survivor Felicia (Ella) Bryn, who had traveled from Florida with members of her family. And in the third row, a woman Lucia's age wept tears of joy, pain, and remembrance. Her hair had thinned and her face had grown drawn with the years, but her eyes still radiated warmth.

It was her first and oldest friend, her beloved Bochnia schoolmate, Marysia. Lucia's mind flashed back in time, rippling across oceans and slicing through the finite constraints of mortal lives and enclosed places. Genowefa and Franciszek; Chmielewski; St. Mikolaj; the gymnazjum Passion service; the Helen Blatt letter, her first visit to a synagogue—*this* synagogue; her arrest and escape; Israel and New York and the Bobover Rav; Herman; family; the Western Wall; Machu Picchu; and a granddaughter who wanted to have her bat mitzvah in Poland.

How different it felt now than the first time she walked into the Tempel Synagogue fifty years earlier. She was so scared then, so confused. Would the girl she was then have recognized the woman she had become? Perhaps, she thought, she just might. Her spirit was freer now, but it was the same spirit.

Marysia embraced Lucia with her soulful gaze. When the service concluded, Lucia extended her hand to Marysia, as Marysia had once done in church.

It was the first time Marysia had ever been inside a Jewish house of worship.

Being here right now—at the Tempel Synagogue— this is *an orbit of light,* Lucia thought.

For Lucia, in the months following the trip to Poland, the contemplation of her life's meaning took on a sharper focus. She found herself reflecting in awe at the arc of her life, at all that had transpired, and at her mysteriously unfolding purpose. Even as she basked in the glow of her granddaughter's growth, the turbulence of her own childhood ascended to the forefront of her consciousness. What was the meaning of *her* childhood?

In this contemplative mindset she wandered into a bookstore one afternoon in August 2011 and found the book with the photograph of the forlorn children in the shadow of a Nazi that prompted her question to God: why had He been removed and not involved during dark and tragic periods on the planet—like those she lived through?

Sixty-six

January 2012
NEW YORK

In January 2012, inspired messages came again to Lucia. First she was moved to write:

My faith and my courage have been strengthened.

Then she was guided to a passage from the Psalms, specifically King David's Psalm 27. The Psalm immediately spoke to her.

The LORD is my light and my salvation; whom shall I fear?

The LORD is the stronghold of my life; of whom shall I be afraid?

When evil-doers came upon me to eat up my flesh, even mine adversaries and my foes, they stumbled and fell.

Though a host should encamp against me, my heart shall not fear; though war should rise up against me, even then will I be confident.

One thing have I asked of the LORD, that will I seek after: that I may dwell in the house of the LORD all the days of my life, to behold the graciousness of the LORD, and to visit early in His temple.

For He concealed me in His pavilion in the day of evil; He hid me in the covert of His tent; He lifted me up upon a rock.

And now shall my head be lifted up above my enemies; and I will offer in His tabernacle sacrifices with trumpet-sound; I will sing praises unto the LORD.

Hear, O LORD, when I call with my voice; be gracious unto me, and answer me.

In Thy behalf my heart hath said: 'Seek ye My face'; Thy face, LORD, will I seek.

Hide not Thy face from me; put not Thy servant away in anger; Thou hast been my help; cast me not off, neither forsake me, O God of my salvation.

For though my father and my mother have forsaken me, the LORD will take me up.

Teach me Thy way, O LORD; and lead me in an even path, because of them that lie in wait for me.

Deliver me not over unto the will of my adversaries; for false witnesses are risen up against me, and such as breathe out violence.

If I had not believed to look upon the goodness of the LORD in the land of the living.

Wait on the LORD; be strong, and let thy heart take courage; wait for the LORD.

Finally, Lucia felt a profound inner call to go to Jerusalem — yet again. With the Middle East in a state of unrest, Mitchell was concerned about such a trip. But Lucia was resolute. She told him, "It's a choice I'm making. I am choosing to continue the work I was meant to do."

So she made plans to go to Jerusalem in September 2012 for the High Holidays.

Sixty-seven

September 2012
JERUSALEM, ISRAEL

L ucia hoped her spiritual work was not the only reason she had been called to Jerusalem. She first visited in 1994, feeling orphaned for a third time after the loss of her husband, and returned home with the hopeful notion that God would soon help her find a companion. Instead, she'd spent nearly two decades with God as her companion, her days and nights devoted to fostering the Divine communication begun at the Wall. Might she now be blessed to find in Jerusalem a soul partner in the flesh?

She was expecting to meet several friends and acquaintances in Jerusalem, but on the day she arrived, she learned that, for various reasons, none of them would be joining her. She entered the hotel dining room that evening, the first night of Rosh Hashanah, and was seated alone at a small round table in the back of the room. Boisterous groups of families surrounded her, chanting blessings over wine and raisin challahs. No one approached her to ask her to join his or her table.

Why did You bring me here? she asked, her eyes raised to the heavens.

No answer came.

The next morning, Lucia entered the Old City from the Jaffa

Gate and tried to ignore the shouts from market vendors hawking their wares to tourists and pilgrims along the narrow passageways. In a few minutes she descended the stairs that led to the open-air plaza leading to the Western Wall.

Upon her approach, she heard a loud shofar blast. It stirred her, as it once had in Istanbul.

As she inched closer to the Wall she felt her right hand rise up and be guided to its stone blocks. As she felt the Divine presence in her midst, her body trembled and a powerful surge of energy coursed through; it entered her hand and burst through her fingers. Now clear direction entered her consciousness:

Make three circles with the hand that is writing My word. Start and end with the shin position.

Lucia traced the circles on the Wall. As she traced the circles, this entered her consciousness:

You will hear My voice. You will see My face. You will transform.

She held her hand to the Wall, allowing it to relax. Then she sensed the eyes of curious worshippers watching her. How long had they been staring at her? Blood rushed to her face. She darted away from the Wall and found herself walking through the crowd, craving solitude.

"Is there a less crowded way to get back to the King David Hotel?" she asked a soldier. "I don't want to walk back through the busy market."

"Not really," he said. "If you go any other way, you'll likely get lost."

Lucia decided to take her chances. Sure enough, she was lost in a matter of minutes. She wandered nervously through the streets of the Jewish quarter, passing several synagogues and *yeshivot*. She paused to glance at a garden of lilies, tulips, and roses. Just ahead of her, she saw a man with a dark Mediterranean complexion standing on an overpass holding a *talit* bag in his hand. He wore a white shirt and pants, and his salt-and-pepper hair stuck out beneath his white *kippah*. He gazed out, seeming to stare at nothing in particular. She considered approaching him for help, but decided against it. A group of Hasidic men passed by and Lucia asked them for direction. They shrugged their shoulders—they did not speak English. As Lucia turned away from them, the man dressed in white, having stepped down from the overpass, approached her.

"I heard you were looking for the Jaffa Gate," he said softly. Lucia nodded. "I am going there as well. I will show you the way."

Lucia was heartened. *It would be nice to have a man like him by my side,* she thought. *Perhaps…could he be the one? Is he the reason I came this way?* The man began walking a step or two ahead of her. She hoped he would turn back to speak with her. But he continued moving forward in silence. Finally they reached the Jaffa Gate. He glanced back at Lucia.

"Do you now know your way?" he asked.

"I do," she said. "*Shannah tovah.*"

She hoped he would linger a bit, or at least return the holiday greetings, but he spun to his right and soon disappeared.

Lucia let out a deep sigh.

The Sabbath that falls between Rosh Hashanah and Yom Kippur is known as Shabbat Shuvah (Sabbath of Return), a time to focus on repentance and the hope for Divine healing and restoration. For Shabbat services, Lucia returned to the Wall, pondering once again why she had been called to Jerusalem.

She went to the same spot where she had stood on Rosh Hashanah. There she again felt the Divine presence and was directed to trace three circles on the surface of the Wall, with shin as the starting and ending points. As she did this, she heard the words within:

You hear My voice. You see My face. You are transformed.

She felt a shiver down her spine, but not the embarrassment she'd experienced on her previous visit when she noticed people watching her. As she walked back to her hotel room, she felt an energy surrounding her—the same energy she'd felt at the Wall. She'd once shuddered at the notion that she might be receiving Divine communication. Yet now, walking back to her hotel, she embraced the sense of awe, the purpose, and the light that she'd been privileged to encounter.

As the Sabbath afternoon faded into darkness, Lucia opened her journal. Reflecting on the events and emotions of the past few days, she was inspired to write:

You heard My voice. You saw My face. You were transformed.

As she sat reading the words she'd just written, she knew that she was supposed to take them with her and return to the Wall for a third time—on Yom Kippur.

At Machu Picchu, she'd been transported into a timeless, dimensionless space that seemed to bridge heaven and earth. She now felt a similar dimensionless present where the human past, present, and future were all imbued with Divine spirit.

On Yom Kippur she returned to the Wall, and once again traced three circles, beginning and ending with the shin position. As she did, she repeated:

You heard My voice. You saw My face. You were transformed.

After she finished, these words came to her:

Engrave the words in your heart.

She slowly walked away from the Wall, placed her hand over her heart, and held it there.

The next morning, her last in Israel, she embarked on a long-planned tour of Jerusalem's Christian sites. Her tour guide was an engaging companion, a Jewish archeologist with a mystical bent. They soon fell into a deep conversation. He was very moved when Lucia shared some of her experiences, and he led her to a small shop where several artifacts were on display.

He told her that months earlier he'd come across an artifact of special significance, and he'd instructed the proprietor to retain it until its intended recipient appeared. Lucia, he felt, was that person. Standing in the little shop before a glass case, he pointed to the artifact, a second or third-century clay oil lamp engraved with mysterious symbols and patterns. Gazing at the ancient artifact, Lucia felt again the now familiar sense of timelessness and Divine presence; something in the lamp seemed to transcend its mere physicality and envelop her in light.

Lucia boarded her plane at Tel Aviv's Ben-Gurion Airport feeling a profound sense of elevation and weariness. She would fly over the once tumultuous European continent that had once been her home, cross the Atlantic Ocean, and arrive at the New York skyline where the Twin Towers once stood. Her carry-on bag, held close, contained the precious items she'd purchased a day earlier: the ancient lamp, a prayer shawl with blue embroidery, a matching *kippah*, and a *mezuzah*, a doorpost containing a scroll of parchment with Biblical text.

Inscribed on the casing of the mezuzah was the letter *shin*, which Lucia stroked with the tip of her third finger.

EPILOGUE

Open your heart to the one I am sending and follow my voice and record my words that have not been written yet. The voice you are hearing is the same as Abraham heard when he was following the road paved by me.

—From Lucia's journal, February 2008

Life journeys rarely have neat endings. Upon her return from Israel in 2012, Lucia continued fostering Divine communication. She has completed several new volumes of material expanding on many of the themes, visions, and symbols contained in these pages, hoping to uncover further clues to some of the mysteries she has encountered on her journey.

In revisiting Klimt's *Portrait of Adele Bloch-Bauer* at the Neue Galerie in New York, and making the connection with the circles in the ancient Judean lamp and the circles she traced on the Western Wall, she has taken yet another significant step forward in a her journey.

But as this book ends, it must be asked: has Lucia's question about God's apparent lack of involvement during the Holocaust, 9/11, and other tragedies been answered?

Like the question of God's existence, it cannot be objectively answered to everyone's satisfaction. But in Lucia's experience, the question *has* been answered to her satisfaction.

"God *was, is,* and always *will* be present in my life," she says. "He was *never* removed."

But if God has always been present, how does she explain her struggles and the suffering of those who lived and died in the Holocaust as well as countless other tragedies?

For many years this question tugged at her. Were the struggles in her life purposeful? Was it part of a necessary plan out of which a spiritual journey arose? Does it speak to the suffering of others?

Lucia's search for answers to these questions continues. The redemptive power of suffering asserted in many religious traditions is not a notion easily embraced, if it should be embraced at all.

In 2012 Lucia and Mitchell attended a synagogue service at Shirat Hanefesh in Chevy Chase, Maryland. Its unique congregation blends multiple religious traditions. Turning to a random page in the prayer book *Siddur Eit Ratzon* by Professor Joseph Rosenstein of Rutgers University, Lucia came upon a passage that captured her most deeply felt sentiments:

> *God is good ... God's blessings are always with us ... but God's power is not always available to us. To make room for human choice, God withdraws from micromanaging the universe and lets the world continue without Divine intervention. Therefore we offer the alternative here of God's* presence *rather than God's* power. *God is always present, always with us, providing us with strength and comfort, guidance and dignity.*

The notion of God's withdrawal to make room for human free will is hardly a new concept. Sages have long postulated the "hiding of God's face." In *Man Is Not Alone*, renowned twentieth century scholar Abraham Joshua Heschel offers a perhaps more palatable perspective: it is not *God* who hides from man, but *man* who hides from God, as reflected in the choices made by Adam and Eve.

In a world where men hide from God, evil and tragedy are bound to occur. Lucia's engagement with the letter shin—the balancing force between good and evil, between heaven and earth—also suggests that battling against evil and overcoming tragedy are an integral part of the world we live in.

Still, at this time there is no definitive answer to the question of *why* God allows evil and tragedy to exist; or why innocents suffer. As Shmuley Boteach writes in *The Fed Up Man of Faith*, "if a beautiful explanation were offered, it would allow us to sleep better at night. But we are not supposed to sleep easier when there is suffering and tragedy in the world." He suggests that by refusing to tolerate evil, and by questioning God as to why He allows it, we actively engage in the betterment of the world God created.

This book is a product of Lucia's efforts to make this a better world. She struggled in the course of her spiritual journey perhaps as much as she did in her volatile childhood. After her daunting journey of faith, loneliness, doubt, disappointment, and fear, she is satisfied with the path her life has taken.

"The Divine communication I received has been a gift," she says. "That gift, I've learned, is meant to be shared. I am an ordinary woman from a small town in Poland, one of many whose lives have been affected by suffering. But at the base of the mountain where both I and the entire mountain shifted, a panoramic view of a new world was presented to me and *others* who were there, just as there were others who witnessed the golden eagle in my dream vision. Perhaps the doors that were opening at the base of the mountain were opening to a world of hope, peace, and love, and a world of unity between peoples. A world embraced by the golden eagle."

Lucia embraces the challenge that lies before her, believing that she has received Divine assurance of His timeless presence, and that more answers will come as her spiritual effort continues. The ongoing violence and conflicts of the world around us can test our belief in God's presence and fill us with doubts that a shift in world consciousness can ever be accomplished. Lucia's life story affirms that such a shift *must* and *will* take place. For what other reason did the Divine create a *human* presence?

Follow Lucia's ongoing journey and visit an online community dedicated to helping build a "temple of love" by empowering individual choices of tolerance, empathy, and understanding at http://theRoseTemple.com.

ACKNOWLEDGEMENTS

Lucia and Mitchell gratefully acknowledge the following people whose encouragement, support, guidance, and expertise have been instrumental in the development of this book.

Rabbi Zalman Schachter-Shalomi, Felicia (Ella) Bryn, and Sonia Klein offered support and reassurance while they were with us. Miriam Ferber and Jody Rowe Staley have been long-time sources of friendship and support. Susan O'Malley, Carol Targoff, Suzy Snyder, and Stuart Kleiman have long offered Mitchell encouragement and friendship.

Lisa Weitzman, beloved daughter and sister, has been steadfast in her support of this work, embracing her own sense of spirit and authenticity along the way. She honored Lucia by naming her daughter Genna after Genowefa Swiatek.

And Beverly Weitzman, Mitchell's devoted wife and mother of Paula and Joshua, has been an enthusiastic supporter of the project from the outset. She has handled matters at home when Mitchell traveled to meet Lucia for interviews, revisions, and research. And she was instrumental in organizing the memorable 2011 Poland trip.

Dr. Haim Cohen, an archeologist and tour guide at the University of Haifa, was an instrumental resource, as was Ivana Zawidzka, curator at the Muzuem of Bochnia and graduate of Jagiellonian University of Krakow and the Papal Academy of Theology.

Robert Lescher, Gay Walley, Doug Childers, Larry Baker, and Terri Schell all offered insightful and expert editorial advice and input.

Jeremy Kay, executive director of the Library of the Holocaust Foundation and publisher of Bartleby Press, was an invaluable resource throughout the publishing process.

Thank you also to Angela Render for her website design.

Published works by Rabbi Irving Greenberg, Carolyn Myss, Julia Cameron, James Carroll, Rodger Kamenetz, Gregg Braden, and Shari Arison have been instrumental sources of learning and inspiration.

To all those whose love, support, deeds, and contributions made this journey and work possible, a heartfelt thank you.

,

Atlanta-Fulton Public Library